A DISCREDITED TAX
The Capital Gains Tax Problem
and Its Solution

Bruce Sutherland · Adrian Beecroft

Cedric Sandford · Ronald Utt

Barry Bracewell-Milnes

Introduction by
John Chown

Edited by
Barry Bracewell-Milnes

Institute of Economic Affairs
1992

First published in September 1992
by
THE INSTITUTE OF ECONOMIC AFFAIRS
2 Lord North Street, Westminster, London SW1P 3LB

© The Institute of Economic Affairs 1992

IEA Readings 38

All rights reserved

ISSN 0305-814X
ISBN 0-255 36309-5

The Institute gratefully acknowledges financial support for its publications programme and other work from a generous benefaction by the late Alec and Beryl Warren.

Printed in Great Britain by
Goron Pro-Print Co. Ltd., Lancing, W. Sussex

Filmset in 'Berthold' Times Roman 11 on 12 point

CONTENTS

page

INTRODUCTION   *John Chown*   ix

1. TAX PHILOSOPHIES IN CONFLICT:
   COMPLEXITIES, ANOMALIES
   AND COMPLIANCE COSTS   *Bruce Sutherland*   1

   1. Introduction   1
   2. The Original Concept of the United Kingdom
      Capital Gains Tax   1
   3. Subsequent Developments   3
      The Rate of Tax   3
      Chargeable Assets   4
      Death   4
      Gifts *Inter Vivos*   4
      Inflation   5
      Pooling   5
      Other   6
   4. Taxpayers' Perception of the Tax   6
      The 1988 Budget   7
   5. The Boundary Argument   8
   6. The Clog on the Market   9
   7. Anomalies   11
   8. Conclusion   13

   ANNEX: *The Interaction Between Capital Gains Tax and Inheritance Tax*   14

2. CAPITAL GAINS TAX AND THE
   ENTERPRISE CULTURE   *Adrian Beecroft*   15

   1. Risk Aversion Rational Under the Present Tax System   15
   2. Two BVCA Surveys   17
   3. Tax Changes have Lengthened the Odds
      Against Successful Entrepreneurs   18

4. Foreign Tax Systems More Favourable to Risk Capital   19
5. Shortage of Seed Capital Caused by Taxation   20
6. The Paradox of Government Policy   21
7. Revenue Gains from Abolishing Capital Gains Tax   22
8. Gains on Unquoted Shares not Analogous to Income   23
9. Recommendations   24

ANNEX I: *Tax and the Manager/Entrepreneur*   25
ANNEX II: *Summary of Taxation Treatment by Country*   26
ANNEX III: *Tax Revenue from Growing Companies*   28

TABLES:
1. Obstacles to Recruitment by Venture Capitalists   17
2. Capital Gains Tax for Entrepreneurs: Tax Rate on
   Long-Term Holdings of Less Than 25% of the Equity
   of the Company, 1989   20

3. CAPITAL GAINS TAXES IN
   OECD COUNTRIES   *Cedric Sandford*   31
   1. Introduction   31
      International Comparisons—'Broad Distinction' Only   32
   2. Why Countries Adopted Capital Gains Tax   34
   3. Short- and Long-Term Gains   34
      The Arguments for Differentiation   35
   4. Treatment of Losses   36
   5. Rates and Thresholds   37
   6. Revenue Yield   37
   7. Treatment of Gains at Death and on Gifts   42
   8. Exemption and Reliefs: The Principal Private Residence   43

TABLES:
1. Main Methods of Taxing the Capital Gains of Private Persons
    as at November 1987   33
2a. Rates and Thresholds, November 1987
    (a) Countries with Separate Capital Gains Tax   38
2b. Rates and Thresholds, November 1987
    (b) Countries with Comprehensive Coverage within
        Income Tax   39-41

Contents

4. EMPIRICAL SUPPORT FOR REDUCING RATES OF
   CAPITAL GAINS TAX IN THE UNITED STATES   *Ronald Utt*   45
   1. Introduction   45
   2. Current Prospects for a Cut in the Rates of Capital Gains Tax   45
      Worsening Budget Deficit   46
   3. Opposition to Lower Rates of Capital Gains Tax   47
   4. The Impact of Capital Taxation on Investment Decisions   48
      What the Data Reveal   48
      Dramatic Increase in Capital Raised Through
         Initial Public Offerings (IPOs)   49
   5. Consequences for the Tax Revenue of Reducing Rates
      of Capital Gains Tax   53
      What the Data Reveal   54
      The Revenue Impact Debate   56
   6. Tax Revenues and Fairness: Who Wins?   57
   7. The Proposals Before Congress   60
      Tax Rates   61
      Holding Period   61
      Coverage   62
   8. Conclusion   63
Other Sources for Capital Gains Tax Reform in the United States   64

TABLES:
   1. New Capital Raised Through Initial Public Stock
      Offerings (IPOs): USA, 1969-1990   50
   2. Supply of Venture Capital Financing: USA, 1969-1990   52
   3. Capital Gains Realisations and Tax Revenues: USA, 1954-1989   55
   4. Percentage Increases in Capital Gains Tax Payments
      by Adjusted Gross Income: USA, 1980-1984   58
   5. Distribution of Capital Gains by Recurring Income:
      USA, 1985   60

5. CAPITAL GAINS TAX:
   REFORM THROUGH ABOLITION   *Barry Bracewell-Milnes*   65
   1. Introduction   65
      Chancellor Lawson's 'horophobia'   66
   2. British Political and Fiscal Background   67
      Further Legislative Changes   68

A Discredited Tax

3. The Statistical Background 69
4. The Academic Background 70
5. The Capital Gains Tax Quandary 72
   Capital Gains Realisations Basis 73
6. The Incidence of Capital Gains Tax 75
7. Capital Gains Tax and its Identity Crisis 77
8. Inequity Between Taxpayers 77
9. Losses Without Gains 80
10. Relationship With Other UK Taxes 81
11. Conclusion and Implications for Policy 82
    (A) Reductions in Capital Gains Tax Compatible
        with its Abolition 84
    (B) Reductions in Capital Gains Tax Compatible
        with its Continued Existence 84
12. Summary 85

THE AUTHORS 87

SUMMARY *Back cover*

INTRODUCTION

John Chown
J. F. Chown & Company Limited

IN IEA READINGS No. 38, *A Discredited Tax: The Capital Gains Tax Problem and Its Solution*, Barry Bracewell-Milnes and his fellow authors examine comprehensively and convincingly the muddle into which our system of capital gains taxation has fallen. The dilemma is simply stated but less easily resolved.

From one point of view, it seems there should be a comprehensive income tax designed to catch income of all types. A broadly based tax with no loopholes and no exceptions can and should be imposed at a low rate. Why should capital gains be excluded? Specifically, why should someone whose skill lies in buying and selling shares (or other 'capital assets') be treated for tax or any other purposes differently from someone who buys and sells cars, computers or cornflakes?

If we look more closely we find that some (Barry Bracewell-Milnes argues most) types of capital gain are not a proper subject for taxation at all. First, and (now) most obviously, purely inflationary gains should surely be exempt. That is an old campaign of mine, substantially won in 1982 subject to a few later skirmishes.

Second, and almost as obviously, gains resulting from a change in stock market conditions should not be taxed. Assume you invest £100,000 to produce gross dividends of £10,000 per annum (10 per cent yield) and (dividend rates remaining unchanged) the market subsequently moves from a 10 per cent yield basis to a 5 per cent yield basis, the value of your assets doubles to £200,000. On paper you are richer but have no more income. With the capital gains tax régime, if you sell shares to adjust your portfolio, you pay tax, leaving less to re-invest, and your income actually falls. What if the market rises because dividends rise? Barry Bracewell-Milnes would argue that, even then, there is no occasion for tax. The higher income will be caught for tax in due course: taxing capital gains either simply anticipates future tax receipts, or taxes the same event twice.

Without going into detail (though the authors do), it is clear that some forms of capital gain can perfectly properly be taxed at full rates, while others should not be taxed at all. Where do we draw the line? Some 'horophobes', as Bracewell-Milnes describes them, say it is so difficult that one should not even try, and argue in favour of taxing everything. They are given short order in this *Readings*. Certainly my own professional experience, which goes back to the original introduction of capital gains tax, confirms that the borderline is a major battleground.

The same experience leads me to conclude that there is no simple philosophically justifiable answer to this, or indeed most, questions of tax policy. A second-best compromise has to be accepted. Taxing gains but at a reduced rate worked reasonably well until 1988. That, rather than abolition, should be our immediate target, accepting that it can be attacked by tax philosophers from both ends. It may well result in some types of gain, such as those from systematic speculation, being rather under-taxed while leaving others over-taxed. Its only justification is that it seems to work.

Cedric Sandford's overview of capital gains taxes in OECD countries gives no comfort to those who think there must be a simple solution. If there is, no country has discovered it and put it into practice. Nevertheless, his chapter demonstrates that some countries may have found a more efficient compromise than others.

In spite of the well-meaning (although in practice disastrous) equalisation of rates in 1988, Britain is still a long way short of a comprehensive tax base. Leaving aside the special treatment of investment intermediaries, gains within pension funds, on owner-occupied houses and on government securities and qualifying corporate bonds are all exempt. (Indeed, the history of the tax treatment of fixed-interest securities and their derivatives is a horror story equal to any told within these pages.)

Furthermore, those who believe in the 'philosophy' of full tax on capital gains should logically bring into account unrealised as well as realised gains. Tax should be imposed on an accruals rather than on a realisations basis, but could that work? I suggested earlier that some argue buying and selling securities should not be distinguished for tax or any other purposes from buying and selling anything else. In fact, for tax purposes, the speculator is far less favourably taxed by a capital gains tax régime. If, as a good trader should, he gears up his transactions with borrowed money, he will be denied tax relief on the interest he pays on his borrowing, although there is a serious mismatch since he is fully taxed on the resulting dividends and capital gains. The general trader computes his taxable profits after deducting interest; if he makes a loss he is permitted to offset it against any other income in the same year, carry it back for three years against past profits, or forward indefinitely. Loss relief on capital gains is very limited indeed, ensuring that the Revenue can collect a substantial yield from the tax in a year when markets collapse and investors as a whole lose money.

Other, more detailed anomalies are discussed by Bruce Sutherland. Although many of the problems he raises could be dealt with by specific amendment to legislation, the tax would become more complex even than it is today. His contribution surely demolishes the hopes of those who seek a truly comprehensive and logical tax base to include both income and gains. There is no such animal.

In the United States, Congress has wasted more breath in the pursuit of the fool's gold of a philosophically perfect tax system than any other legislature in the world. It has also meddled with capital gains and other taxes most frequently. Whatever this hyperactivity does to the country, it makes it a superb laboratory for the study of the practical effects of capital gains taxation. Ronald Utt summarises the huge volume of empirical evidence available. This shows clearly that high rates of capital gains tax, particularly as in the USA where applying to unindexed gains, can do serious damage to the real economy (particularly its more entrepreneurial parts). The evidence also establishes that there is a fairly low rate of tax which maximises the total revenue from capital gains tax. The figure is somewhere between 9 and 22 per cent and has certainly varied over time because of several factors, including the rate of inflation and the tax régime applying to regular income. At some figure, well short of that applying in the UK, every increase in the rate of the tax actually inhibits transactions to the point of reducing the total tax take. The

1986 US tax reform, with its move towards lower rates and a broader base was, in general concept, eminently sensible, but defects in the treatment of capital gains and of profits distributed by companies precipitated two disasters, both of which were predictable and predicted. It virtually killed the venture capital industry, and gave rise to the wild excesses (and subsequent collapse) of the junk bond boom.

Venture capital is the theme of Adrian Beecroft's contribution. He is particularly concerned to analyse the risk/reward ratio facing an executive considering a move from a large public to a small private company. The fall in immediate income and in long-term security has to be balanced by the prospect of a substantial long-term capital gain. The prospect of paying 40 per cent tax on that gain can tilt the odds decisively against the move. The deterrent effect on entrepreneurship is undoubtedly the most important way in which high capital gains taxes can damage the real economy.

The point may appear a little over-stated. Shareholding executives of private companies can, with good advice, retain a fair portion of the fruits of their toil. They can set up money purchase pension funds as effectively as public company executives, and often with more control over how the money is invested. They can optimise between dividends (no national insurance), salaries and bonuses (national insurance, but can enhance the level of pension contributions), pension contributions (very efficient) and eventual capital gains (retirement relief). They can get tax relief on interest on money borrowed to invest, generous relief on losses on private company shares, and 100 per cent inheritance tax exemption. But why should they need specialist advice when they can least afford it? Why not have a simple, easily understood régime?

Seen in that light, the business expansion scheme was a disaster. 'BES funds', property-related deals and the like should never have been allowed. What should have been a good idea fell into the hands of commission-driven salesmen of 'financial products'. What was required was to encourage funding put together at local level between entrepreneurs and investors known to each other, and with both enjoying a measure of tax relief. Maybe, apart from anything else, it was doomed by the complexities of the Financial Services Act. The whole subject of the tax treatment of private companies and how to encourage entrepreneurship is complex. Capital gains tax is an important part but not the only part of the problem.

Each of the authors has looked at the problem from a different point of view, identified different problems and proposed slightly different solutions. If there is a consensus, it is probably towards retaining the capital gains tax but at a much lower rate. The Revenue take certainly seems to fall off after the introduction of some low rate—15 per cent, or perhaps 20 per cent—and we should certainly ensure that no capital gain is taxed at a higher rate than that. Given that incremental revenue falls, and economic damage increases with every percentage point on the rate, the economic optimum must be lower than the rate which maximises revenue. It may even be zero.

With a low rate, what other reliefs do we need? I would keep indexation, even though it *should* become irrelevant.[1]

August 1992   JOHN CHOWN
                                                              J. F. Chown & Co. Limited

*   *   *

The views expressed in this *IEA Readings*, edited by Barry Bracewell-Milnes, are of course those of the authors and not those of the Institute (which has no corporate view), its Trustees, its Directors or its Advisers. The Institute publishes this *Readings* as a contribution to the debate on tax policy which has significant implications for Britain's economic performance.

C.R.

---

[1] In the late 1970s, it was argued that indexation perpetuated inflation. I distinguished between 'virtuous indexation' (which stripped from government the profits of inflation) and 'vicious indexation' which protected civil service pensions, for instance, which benefitted those in government and simply encouraged them.

TAX PHILOSOPHIES IN CONFLICT

– Complexities, Anomalies and Compliance Costs

Bruce Sutherland

1. Introduction

THIS PAPER EXAMINES and comments on:

○ the original concept of the United Kingdom capital gains tax, which was the work of the late Lord Kaldor, the author of the Memorandum of Dissent to the 1955 Report of the Royal Commission on the Taxation of Profits and Income;

○ the major developments in the tax since its introduction in 1965;

○ the 'boundary argument' which seeks to justify taxing gains as if they were income;

○ the effect of the tax on markets; and

○ some of the anomalies in the charge to the tax;

and sets out the conclusions arrived at from that examination.

2. The Original Concept of the UK Capital Gains Tax

The Royal Commission on the Taxation of Profits and Income in its *Final Report* in June 1955 (Cmd.9474) recommended that capital gains should not be brought into the charge to income tax nor into a charge to a flat-rate tax (Chapter 4).

Three members of the Royal Commission, Messrs. Woodcock, Bullock and Kaldor, entered a Memorandum of Dissent to this and other recommendations. Most of the recommendations contained in the Memorandum of Dissent were adopted and enacted in the first Budget of the new Labour Government in 1965 and, in particular, those relating to corporation tax and capital gains tax.

The rationale of the new capital gains tax can be summarised in the following quotations from the Memorandum of Dissent:

(i) 'In fact, no concept of income can be really equitable that stops short of the comprehensive definition which embraces all receipts which increase an individual's command over the use of society's scarce resources – in other words, his "net accretion of economic power between two points of time" ' (para. 5).

(ii) 'In applying the basic conception of income as the power to satisfy material needs to any workable tax system, a number of guiding principles need to be introduced.

(1) The first of these is, in the words of the Majority, that "no income [should be] recognised as arising unless an actual receipt has taken place, although a receipt may take the form of a benefit having money's worth received in kind as well as of money or of a payment made to a third party in discharge of another's legal debt".

(2) The second guiding principle is that receipts which cannot reasonably be brought within the scope of taxation because their control and enforcement is beyond the power of any efficient tax administration are better ignored altogether. ... (Gambling winnings may be regarded as an example of this.) The obvious corollary to this principle is that outlays or expenses chargeable against gross receipts which cannot be efficiently and uniformly administered ... should similarly be ignored.

(3) Thirdly, under a progressive system of taxation, recognition needs to be given to the fact that unique or non-recurrent receipts obtained in any particular period do not confer the same spending power on the recipient within that period as recurrent receipts of like amount.' (para. 8)

(iii) 'On the other hand there are circumstances in which a tax on realised gains inevitably involves a bunching of gains in time, and hence, under a progressive tax, would involve the taxpayer in heavier liability owing to the incidence of timing. This would obviously occur where the capital profits are derived from a single indivisible asset – as for example when a man who has gradually built up a business sells it as a going concern or it changes hands at his decease. But it may occur more generally in cases where the capital assets are not easily marketable and can only be realised infrequently or when a wholesale realisation of accrued but unrealised gains is deemed to have occurred through death. This familiar problem in equity under progressive taxation arises in connection with capital gains whenever a property owner is not in a position to spread out or regulate the realisation of his net capital profits. It should be emphasised that the problem disappears under a flat-rate tax, and that it constitutes the main argument, in equity, for a flat rate rather than a progressive rate of tax on capital gains.'

'Independently of the above consideration we recognise the force of the argument which leads to the conclusion that it would be inexpedient to tax capital gains at the full progressive rate of income tax and surtax combined. ... If capital gains were subjected to both income tax and surtax the effect would be that a great part of these gains would be taxed at an extremely high rate (amounting at present to 19s 0d in the £) which would be bound to have a destructive effect on the willingness to assume risks. Added to this is the consideration that since a great deal of capital investment is made in the expectation of distant and not immediate appreciation even those investors not currently liable to the higher surtax rates would be in considerable uncertainty as to the rate at which their ultimate gains would be taxed when realised. Finally the full charging of capital gains to both income tax and surtax would have a negative effect on the incentive to save and encourage capitalists to dissipate their capital. ... We think therefore that the taxation of capital gains beyond a certain rate would have highly undesirable effects on risk-bearing, saving and capital formation.'

'We therefore recommend that subject to the qualifications and on the definitions suggested below capital gains should be subjected to income taxation but not to surtax.' (paras. 60, 61 and 62)

3. Subsequent Developments

The Rate of Tax

The Memorandum of Dissent to the 1955 Royal Commission Report recommended that capital gains should be charged to income tax but not to surtax. When the tax was introduced in 1965, the standard rate of tax

3

was fixed at 41.25 per cent (up from 38.75 per cent for the previous year). However, the flat rate at which capital gains were to be charged was fixed at 30 per cent. This was because the arguments against subjecting capital gains to progressive taxation (see (iii) above) were considered sufficiently strong to justify the imposition of a rate of tax significantly lower than even the standard rate of income tax.

In spite of this, as the standard, later basic, rates of income tax have fallen over the years, successive governments have failed to make corresponding reductions in the rate of capital gains tax.

From 1987 the capital gains of companies, which had, until then, been charged at the same rate as those of individuals, 30 per cent, were subjected to corporation tax at the same rate as profits and other income, that is to say, at rates between 25 and 37.75 per cent depending on the amount of the company's profits and/or other income.

From 1988 the capital gains of individuals, trustees, etc., became chargeable to tax at the marginal rate of income tax which would be payable if the gains were additional income of the year of assessment in which they arose.

Chargeable Assets

In 1969 British Government securities became exempt from the tax, because the Treasury and managers of the market in them considered that the charge to capital gains tax was a clog on the market and inhibited its efficient management and that of government debt.

Death

Under the original provisions, death was an occasion of charge and property passing on death was charged as if it had been disposed of at probate value. The capital gains tax charged on the deemed disposal was allowed as a deduction for estate duty purposes. The property, which passed on the death, was acquired for capital gains tax purposes by the persons to whom it passed at probate value.

In 1971 the charge on death was repealed but the property which passed on death continued to be treated as acquired by the persons to whom it passed at probate value.

Gifts *Inter Vivos*

Under the original provisions, gifts were generally treated as disposals, chargeable to capital gains tax by reference to the open market value of the subject matter at the time of the gift.

In 1978 relief was given in respect of gifts of business assets – in general interests in proprietorships, partnerships and controlled companies, engaged in trades and professions, and in assets owned by the taxpayer and used in such businesses. The relief took the form of permitting the gain on the disposal to be held over and deducted from the market value at the time of the gift so that the donee in effect acquired the subject matter at the donor's original cost.

In 1980 hold-over relief, similar to that in relation to business assets, was extended to all gifts by individuals and in 1981 and 1982 to gifts to settlements and distributions out of settlements to beneficiaries.

In 1989 the hold-over relief for gifts, other than those of business assets, was withdrawn.

Inflation

When the capital gains tax was introduced in 1965, inflation for the previous 10 years had averaged 3 per cent per annum. Although there were a few who voiced concern about the threat to the social fabric presented by continuing inflation at that level, the great majority regarded such inflation as an acceptable price which had to be paid for continuing growth in the standard of living. Certainly it was not generally perceived as requiring any allowance for its effects in the new capital gains tax. Compensation for inflation was not the motive for the removal of government securities from the charge in 1969 (see 'Chargeable Assets', above, p.4).

In the five years after 1965, inflation rose to an average 4.5 per cent per annum and thereafter it escalated, peaking at well over 20 per cent in 1975.

From the mid-1970s, the representative bodies of the professions, industry and commerce urged governments to give relief for the effects of inflation on the tax. It was not, however, until 1982 that relief was given and then only for inflation arising after March of that year. Finally, in 1988 the tax was rebased from 31 March 1982, at which date all assets then held could be treated as acquired at their then market value. However, the price exacted for this was the treatment of all gains realised thereafter as if they were income (see above, p.4).

Pooling

Shares and other securities present peculiar problems in a capital gains tax regime because a holding at any time of a single class of shares of a particular company can be the result of a series of purchases and perhaps sales over many years. When the tax was introduced in 1965, rules had to be made for the identification of those shares, etc., acquired before and those acquired after 5 April in that year which were deemed to be comprised in a subsequent disposal. When the indexation allowance was introduced in 1982, the problem was compounded. The re-basing of the tax to 31 March 1982, inevitably compounded it still further. As a result, the provisions in the legislation providing for different 'pools' of shares are complex in the extreme. It also leads to what taxpayers understandably perceive to be injustice in certain circumstances (see the case of Mr S. described below, p.13).

Other

There have been minor changes to the tax in most years since its introduction. There has been no discernible pattern in these changes, apart from those made to correct abuses perceived, or imagined, by the Inland Revenue. Capital gains tax was the subject of what is probably the most contentious judgement of the House of Lords in any case in the history of UK taxation.[1]

4. Taxpayers' Perception of the Tax

Adam Smith laid great emphasis on the importance of ensuring that, so far as possible, tax should be perceived by taxpayers to be fair and reasonable and should be so designed as to minimise harmful disturbances to the economy.

In two areas in particular the history of the UK capital gains tax demonstrates failure to recognise this principle on the part of the Inland Revenue and of Treasury Ministers. The first was the protracted resistance by Inland Revenue officials to the introduction of relief for inflation, on the grounds of the legislative and administrative problems which it was alleged this would involve. The second was the change in 1988 from a tax at a flat rate, significantly lower originally than the standard rate of income tax, to one levied at the rates of income tax which would apply if the gains were additional income of the taxpayer in the year of assessment in which they are realised; for most taxpayers, this means a rate of charge significantly higher than the basic rate of income tax.

---

[1] Furniss v. Dawson ((1984) 1, All E.R., 530.)

The 1988 Budget

In his 1988 Budget speech, the Chancellor of the Exchequer, Nigel Lawson, said:

'Rebasing the tax so as to produce a fully indexed system makes it possible to bring the taxation of gains closer to that of income. In principle there is little economic difference between income and capital gains, and many people effectively have the option of choosing to a significant extent which to receive. And, insofar as there is a difference, it is by no means clear why one should be taxed more heavily than the other.

'Taxing them at different rates distorts investment decisions and inevitably creates a major tax avoidance industry. Moreover, at present, with capital gains taxed at 30 per cent for everybody, higher rate taxpayers face a lower – sometimes much lower – rate of tax on gains than on investment income, while basic rate taxpayers face a higher rate of tax on gains than on income.

'This contrast is hard to justify. I therefore propose a fundamental reform. Subject to the new base date, capital gains will continue to be worked out as now, with the present exemptions and reliefs. ... But the indexed gain will be taxed at the income tax rate that would apply if it were the taxpayer's marginal slice of income.

'In other words, I propose in future to apply the same rate of tax to income and capital gains alike. ... Taxing capital gains at income tax rates makes for greater neutrality in the tax system. It is what we now do for companies. And it is also the practice in the United States, with the big difference that there they have neither indexation relief nor a separate capital gains threshold.'

It may be noted here that the top rate of income tax in the United States was 33 per cent, slightly higher than the previous rate of capital gains tax in the UK, but significantly lower than the 40 per cent top rate in the UK. The great majority of fiscs subject capital gains to a lower rate of tax than income. Some, like the UK before 1965 (or 1962 in the matter of short-term gains), do not seek to tax gains at all.

Mr Lawson's words above, 'In principle there is little economic difference between income and capital gains', echo those of the late Lord Kaldor in the Memorandum of Dissent to the 1955 Royal Commission Report:

7

'In fact no concept of income (as a tax base) can be really equitable that stops short of the comprehensive definition which embraces all receipts which increase an individual's command over the use of society's scarce resources – in other words his "net accretion of economic power between two points of time".'

However, in that Memorandum of Dissent, it was recognised that there is in fact a significant difference between capital gains and income (see above, pp.2-3). *This is the perception of taxpayers* and, indeed, of many economists. In this case, however, what matters is not the theories of economists, however cogently argued, but the perceptions of taxpayers. A necessary prerequisite of the realisation of a gain is generally the investment of capital and its exposure to risk. If it is capital derived from savings out of taxed income, the taxpayer may well perceive it not to be a proper subject for further taxation. It is further widely perceived that the tax strikes not so much at the already rich but rather at those seeking to become rich. This assessment is reinforced by the fact that the charge to inheritance tax on modest estates was, and is, heavier than estate duty after the increases introduced by Sir Stafford Cripps in 1949, and even heavier than capital transfer tax under Mr Healey's 'squeeze the rich' Budget in 1974.[2] The inevitable reaction of taxpayers to the levying of tax on capital gains, as if they were income, is an increased propensity to seek to avoid, and even to evade, the tax. Unacceptably high rates of taxes on both income and capital have deeply eroded taxpayers' morality since 1945. It is notable that a Government which has done so much since 1979 to restore acceptability to the tax system, should have marred its record in this way.

5. The Boundary Argument[3]

The conventional wisdom of those who support a capital gains tax on the United States model was stated in Mr Lawson's 1988 Budget Speech (see above, p.7). No doubt Mr Lawson was persuaded to 'remove the boundary' by such arguments and by promises from the Inland Revenue that this would enable the tax system to be simplified.

---

[2] These relationships have held good for many years. The scale of March 1991 exceeded the 1949 scale on estates from some £150,000 to £850,000 in 1991 prices, imposing just twice as much tax (£24,000 instead of £12,000) on an estate of £200,000. The March 1991 scale was slightly above even the harsh Healey scale of 1974 for estates from some £250,000 to £400,000. The relationships still held good at the 1992 Election, all figures being 5 per cent higher.

[3] The boundary argument is considered further in Chapter 5 by Barry Bracewell-Milnes, below, pp.72-73.

Of course it did not. We have not seen the repeal of any of the numerous provisions in the taxing acts aimed at 'boundary-crossing' devices. Indeed, we have had, and shall continue to have, added complexities resulting from the change, of which Schedule 10 to the Finance Act 1988 was merely the first instalment and the close investment companies saga in the 1989 Finance Bill the second.

It is ironic that the Memorandum of Dissent to the Royal Commission's Report itself recognised that it is 'inexpedient' to charge gains as if they were income (para.61). Those arguments are still valid, even though the top rate of income tax is no longer the ridiculous one charged in 1955.

6. The Clog on the Market

Under the original charging provisions in the Finance Act 1965, government securities were chargeable assets. In 1969 they became exempt, because the Treasury and the managers of the market in these securities considered that the charge to capital gains tax was a clog on the market and inhibited its efficient operation. The potential for gains on money stocks is severely limited. The market for equities must be inhibited to a much greater extent than was the market in gilts by a tax charged in most cases at 40 per cent, as compared with 30 per cent in 1969.

Consider the charge to tax on an individual who bought, or was deemed to acquire, the All Share Index on 31 March 1982 and sold it on 31 August 1989:

'Proceeds'		
All Share Index at 31 August 1989		1,207.45
'Cost'		
All Share Index at 31 March 1982	326.59	
Indexation allowance 0.458	149.58	
		476.17
Chargeable gain		731.28
Tax at 40 per cent		292.51
as percentage of gross proceeds		24.2%
as percentage of monetary gain (1,207.45 – 326.59)		33.2%

Paragraph 68 of the Memorandum of Dissent to the Royal Commission Report states:

'We agree with the Majority that in times of inflation a tax on capital gains would inflict hardship on the owner-occupier who for personal or business reasons has to sell his house and find a new home somewhere else, and who may need all the money received from the sale of his old house for the purchase of another house of the same quality and condition. If the scope of the capital gains tax were extended to the case of the owner-occupier this might have the further undesirable effect of hindering mobility since people might be deterred from accepting new jobs if it meant that they had to sell their existing home. We therefore recommend that the gains arising out of the sale of owner-occupied houses, to the extent of one residence for each taxpayer, should be exempted from the capital gains tax.'

But this argument is similarly valid for shares. The individual taxpayer who owns the All Share Index would undoubtedly say that a tax which confiscates 24.2 per cent of the total proceeds or 33.2 per cent of his monetary gain 'inflicts hardship on him'. It should go without saying that, except in the most unusual circumstances, he will not be able to find an alternative investment on which he can expect to make an almost immediate gain of 32 per cent (24.2 per cent as a percentage of 75.8) to restore his capital position.

It follows that there must be very substantial amounts of equity investments, and indeed of other types of asset, which the owners feel they cannot change or sell, however much such a course of action would be prudent for commercial or other reasons in a tax-neutral context. Commercial decisions are distorted by tax considerations. The new tax does not 'make for greater neutrality in the tax system', as Mr Lawson asserted (above, p.7), but for less.

Holdings of quoted investments by individuals have fallen as a percentage of the total throughout the post-war period. The reasons for this, apart from death duties in their various forms, have been the excessively high levels of taxation on the income and capital of individuals for much of the period and the substantial tax advantages enjoyed by institutionalised investment by comparison with investment by individuals. Contributions to pension funds are tax deductible and the income and gains of such funds are wholly exempt from tax. Life assurance, unit trusts and investment trusts have, to a greater or lesser extent, enjoyed favourable tax regimes for capital gains over most of the period. The imposition of tax on the capital gains of individuals, as if they were additional income, can only stimulate this trend which for a variety of reasons is widely regarded as undesirable.

7. Anomalies

There will always be anomalies in any tax system. The examples below, however, have all been pointed out to Treasury Ministers and Inland Revenue officials, in some cases for many years, without any action having been taken to put them right.

o If an individual makes an outright gift in specie in his lifetime, he pays capital gains tax on the excess of the value of the subject matter over its indexed cost or 1982 value. If he dies within seven years thereafter, he pays inheritance tax on the value of the gift and, if within three years, without abatement. Had he retained the subject matter, it would pass on death at its value free of capital gains tax. There is set out in the annex to this paper (below, p.14) an example of the effect of this anomaly.

o Where there is no interest in possession (entitlement to income) in settled property, income tax is charged at 35 per cent. Where there is an interest in possession, income tax is charged at 25 per cent. In a settlement where there is an interest in possession in part of the settled property, the income arising from that part is only charged at 25 per cent and the income from the part in which there is no interest in possession is charged at 35 per cent. In such a case, however, all capital gains on any part of the settled property are charged at 35 per cent.

o Individuals and trustees of settled property have an annual exemption whereby, in 1992-93, the first £5,800 or £2,900 respectively of their capital gains in any year escape the charge to tax.

   (i) No such exemption is given to companies, not even to close investment companies.

   (ii) Although, as has been pointed out to the Inland Revenue, it would involve little or no administrative difficulty, there is no provision whereby individuals or trustees who have 'lumpy' assets, such as land or an interest in a private business, can carry forward unused annual exemptions to set against the gains on the ultimate realisation of such assets. The portfolio investor can and does 'bed and breakfast' gains up to the amount of the exemption each year. The system is much more favourable to the portfolio investor.

o Losses can be set against gains only in the same or subsequent years of assessment and, if made on a transaction with a connected person, only against gains on further transactions with that connected person. The effect of the above is:

(i) to inhibit lifetime gifts and gifts of assets, the value of which is less than their indexed cost;

(ii to penalise trusts in which part only, however small, of the settled property is not subject to interests in possession;

(iii)to penalise the owners of non-fungible assets;

(iv)to penalise any taxpayers unfortunate or foolish enough to suffer losses later than gains, rather than the other way round, unless they have further assets which can be disposed of to produce chargeable gains.

The most significant of the effects described above is the first one. In 1986 gifts to individuals and to accumulation and maintenance trusts were exempted from the charge to capital transfer tax (which was in consequence renamed the inheritance tax), provided that the donor survived the gift by seven years. In 1987 the relief was extended to gifts to interest-in-possession trusts. The reason for these exemptions was to encourage lifetime gifts. Only two years later, in 1989, the ability to hold over the tax on chargeable gains on all except qualifying business assets was removed. In many, if not most, cases the charge to capital gains tax on gifts will be greater than the charge to inheritance tax at lifetime rates would have been. Quite apart from the first anomaly described in Anomalies above (p.11), therefore, these measures, introduced by the same Chancellor of the Exchequer within three years, display a remarkable inconsistency in tax philosophy. The reason for the 1989 change was said by Mr Lawson to be:

'This [the general hold-over relief for gains] was introduced by my predecessor in 1980, when there was still capital transfer tax on lifetime gifts, in order to avoid a form of double taxation. But the tax on lifetime gifts has since been abolished, and the relief is increasingly used as a form of tax avoidance.'

This statement is at best ingenuous. The charge on lifetime gifts had not been abolished but only potentially removed, provided the donor survived seven years. Moreover, for as long as taxes have existed on property passing on death, the avoidance of these taxes has been an incentive to the making of lifetime gifts. It was not, as is implied above, a new phenomenon which had only appeared since the abolition of the tax on lifetime gifts in 1986.

It is also an integral characteristic of the present capital gains tax that the amount of tax levied can exceed the gain. An example will illustrate this point. Mr S acquired 800 shares in a rights issue at 850 pence and sold them a fortnight later at 920 pence, a profit of £560 less dealing costs. Under the CGT averaging or pooling system, the acquisition cost was deemed to be, not what he paid, but the average acquisition cost of his whole shareholding, most of which he had acquired years earlier when the price was much lower (200). His tax liability was over £2,500 on a profit of under £500.

8. Conclusion

Capital gains tax is inefficient in that the taxpayers affected regard it, with good reason, as being charged at unacceptably high rates.

The tax is inequitable in that the amount of tax levied can exceed the amount realised on a disposal.

The tax is complex and the complexities have been, and probably will be, increased, not reduced, by the removal of the boundary between it and income tax.

The tax is a significant clog on the efficient working of the markets, in particular on those in land and equity shares.

The tax inhibits investment in chargeable assets and the dispersion of wealth by gifts.

The tax tilts still further the bias towards indirect investment through institutions and against direct investment by individuals.

The tax raises comparatively little revenue: the excess, if any, of that revenue over what it would be at acceptable rates does not justify the distortions in the economy and the tax-reducing actions of taxpayers which it causes. Indeed, experience both here and in the United States indicates that reduction of the rate of tax to an acceptable level would increase the yield. It is suggested that an acceptable level would be not more than 20 per cent. Professor Laurence Lindsey has estimated that the optimum rate for raising revenue falls within the range from 9-21 per cent, which suggests a rate of 15 per cent.[4]

The abolition of the tax would have beneficial effects on the economy.

'All taxes upon the transference of property of any kind, so far as they diminish the capital value of the property, tend to diminish the

---

[4] See Chapter 4, below, pp.45-64.

funds available for productive labour. They are all more or less unthrifty taxes that increase the revenue of the sovereign which seldom maintains any but unproductive labourers, at the expense of the capital of the people, which maintains nothing but productive.' (Adam Smith, *Wealth of Nations*, Book V, Chapter II, Part 2, Appendix to Articles 1 and 2.)

ANNEX

The Interaction Between Capital Gains Tax and Inheritance Tax

Assume that an individual gives away the All Share Index, as on pp.9-10 above, and dies the next day, leaving his estate to the donee of the gift. Assume further that the value does not change between the two days. The tax consequences would be:

Value of gift	1,207.45
Capital gains tax thereon	292.51
Net addition to estate on death	914.94
Inheritance tax at 40 per cent	365.98
Capital gains tax as above	292.51
Total tax suffered	£658.49
As a percentage of the gift	55%

Had he not made the gift, the tax payable on his death on the value of the subject matter, £1,207.45, would have been 40 per cent, or £482.98.

It should be noted that, even when the gains on gifts could be held over, so that the donee acquired the liability to the donor's chargeable gain to date on the former's ultimate disposal of the subject matter, this anomaly applied, albeit to a lesser extent, according to the length of the period of time which elapsed before the donee realised the subject matter by sale. Thus, it also still applies in those cases where gains can still be held over, that is, to gifts of qualifying business assets and those which are subject to a lifetime charge to inheritance tax.

2

CAPITAL GAINS TAX AND THE ENTERPRISE CULTURE

Adrian Beecroft
Chairman,
British Venture Capital Association

WHY DOES BRITAIN spawn so many great inventions and then fail to realise their potential? Many a book has been written about this question, to which there is no simple answer. However, there is one major factor: the failure to attract high quality management and substantial investment into the small companies where so many of these inventions begin. Television, the micro-processor, the personal computer: all created by individuals or tiny companies, not by industrial giants. Whatever the reason, the culture of big companies suppresses radical innovation. Major new industries begin with small companies. But over the years, in Britain, small companies have failed to attract the management talent and the investment necessary to turn them into big companies. Yet money is not in short supply in Britain, and management talent, if thinner on the ground than it should be, is not scarce. The problem is that the management talent and the money have not been attracted into small companies. Management talent still resides almost exclusively in big companies.

1. Risk Aversion Rational Under the Present Tax System

Venture capitalists often say there are three important things about any deal. These are management, management and ... management. Venture capitalists in general have no shortage of start-up or early-stage deals. But there is a desperate shortage of experienced, successful executives who are prepared to leave the comfort and security of a big company to start a business of their own or to join a young start-up. Hence the tendency for venture capitalists to put an increasing part of their funds into large management buy-outs.

It needs to be emphasised that we are not just thinking about managing directors. Most businesses start with a single person. After some time a layer of management is added. If the business is doubling in size every year, most of that layer needs replacing after two years. People generally cannot develop their own skills to match the growth of the job. The man you hire as finance director of a £2 million company will probably be out of his depth two years later when it is an £8 million company. Venture capitalists spend a great deal of their time trying to help small companies to recruit good management – finance directors, technical directors, marketing directors and sales directors as well as managing directors – from large companies. We know, from bitter experience, how difficult it is. Small companies are risky. Executives have wives, children and mortgages to think about. There are a few well-publicised examples of very well paid executives in Britain, but the vast majority of senior and middle management are not in any way wealthy. In addition to greater risk and longer hours, the small company generally offers lower pay. The carrot is the capital gain from equity in the business. A few years ago you could swap income taxed at 83 per cent or 98 per cent for potential capital gains at 30 per cent. Today marginal income is taxed at 40 per cent, and so are capital gains in theory, although the inadequacy of relief for capital losses means that the effective rate of tax on capital gains is significantly higher than 40 per cent. Indexation of capital gains tax for price rises means that low-risk investments are protected, whereas high-risk investments are taxed at 40 per cent if successful and may generate unrelieved tax losses if unsuccessful. In the long run low income tax should result in a pool of executives who have saved enough to be able to risk joining a small company. But in the short term it is very much harder to get people out of big companies into little ones than it used to be. It is not that executives do not do the sums. On the contrary. There are indeed some who crave independence and would leave a big company even if capital gains tax was 100 per cent. But the vast majority are economically rational, as has been shown in two separate pieces of research commissioned by the British Venture Capital Association (BVCA).

2. Two BVCA Surveys

A survey of members of the BVCA in 1988 produced some fascinating statistics about what happens when venture capitalists try to recruit senior managers from large companies into small ones. The results, compiled from the responses of 37 member-firms, were as follows:

○ On 351 occasions, venture capitalists attempted to recruit managers from large corporations for small businesses. They were successful on 158 occasions (45 per cent).

○ On average, remuneration dropped from £45,000-£50,000 per annum to £33,000-£40,000 per annum, a decrease of approximately 20 per cent. The loss of fringe benefits associated with employment by a big company made the real decrease much larger. Particularly important in this context is the value of the executive's pension rights.

○ The investment made by each manager varied considerably. The average was generally in the range of £10,000 to £30,000, though a number of managers invested over £100,000.

○ In the cases where the venture capitalists were not successful in recruiting a manager, the reasons, where these could be assessed, broke down as shown in Table 1.

Table 1

OBSTACLES TO RECRUITMENT
BY VENTURE CAPITALISTS

Importance of:	Serious	Moderate	No Problem	No Opinion
	%	%	%	%
Possible gain did not justify risk	50	25	17	8
Cut in salary	25	33	25	17
Loss of value of pension	8	50	25	17

The key feature of the survey is that neither the cut in salary nor the loss of value of pension rights is the most important factor in deterring the executive from making the change. The real deterrent is the belief that the possible financial gain arising from the ultimate sale of the executive's shareholding in the small company did not seem to him to justify the risks involved. Half of the managers felt that this was a serious factor in making their decision, while only a quarter felt that the immediate cut in salary was the dominant problem. Clearly the elimination of capital gains tax on such entrepreneurial gains would, by increasing the likely gain by 67 per cent (at today's CGT rate of 40 per cent) change the balance between risk and reward enough to convince a much larger proportion of managers to take the plunge.

Another study was carried out for the BVCA in 1988, by MORI, which showed that 66 per cent of the chief executives interviewed who had thought of setting up their own business had calculated the potential capital gain. Ninety-six per cent of those who had not thought of leaving a big company said that they would calculate the gain if they were approached to join a small business. Forty-eight per cent of the former group and 66 per cent of the latter said that the impact of capital gains would be important or crucial in their decision-making, and nearly half of each group said that they viewed the recent rise in capital gains tax as crucial or important.

3. Tax Changes Have Lengthened the Odds Against Successful Entrepreneurs

Annex I (below, p.25) helps to explain why would-be entrepreneurs are so tax conscious, and why the tax changes since 1979 have had such a damaging impact on enterprise. It is based on the assumption that a manager has the chance to join a young business with a 5 per cent stake. He has to take a 50 per cent pay cut (allowing for the reduction in actual salary plus fringe benefits lost) from £60,000 to £30,000. The lost income after tax is assumed to be invested at 9 per cent net. At 1979 tax rates the manager would have to believe that the company would be worth just £0.942 million or more in five years for him not to lose financially by joining it. He would be four times better off if the company was worth £3.76 million in five years. At 1991 tax rates, however, the company has to be worth £3.9 million for him to break even, and a massive £15.6 million for him to be four times better off.

Experience shows that managers need to believe that they will make roughly four times as much capital gain as the income they would lose before they will consider undertaking the risks and stresses of a small company. The majority of managers interviewed in the MORI poll said that they would need to be between £250,000 and £750,000 better off in five years' time before they would consider leaving their large company. Given that very few start-up companies are ever going to be worth more than £5 million, it is no wonder that it is so unusual nowadays for successful managers to start or join small companies.

These figures show that the higher capital gains tax is, both absolutely and relatively to income tax, the fewer the managers who will leave the steady, boring giants and join the vital, innovative young companies that should be the future of the economy. It must be remembered too that managers also think about what they expect tax rates to be: at least until the 1992 General Election, they have expected capital gains tax to be 50 per cent or more at some point over the next 10 years: probably at the point when they will be wanting to cash in. In a wide range of unquoted companies, including mature companies, the former incentive to re-invest profits in the company with an eye to eventual capital gains has been replaced by an incentive to maximise current extractions in the form of salaries or dividends.

4. Foreign Tax Systems More Favourable to Risk Capital

Mention has been made of the executive who would leave the big company to set up his own business regardless of the capital gains tax rate. The same argument is often used about the born entrepreneur. Two points need to be made about these characters. First, the world is not black and white. Some people are dyed-in-the-wool big company men. Some people are born entrepreneurs. In between there is a whole spectrum of people whose behaviour is influenced by economic factors including tax rates. Any rise in capital gains tax relatively to income tax stifles enterprise.

Secondly, we no longer live on an island. Businessmen of the sort venture capitalists are interested in are international. They know that capital gains tax rates for entrepreneurs are lower in the USA and virtually every European country than they are in the UK. Table 2 is taken from a study carried out by Arthur Andersen for the BVCA and completed in 1989. It shows that in France, Germany, Italy and Holland an entrepreneur generally pays no capital gains tax on the sale of shares in the company that he runs or helps to manage. In the USA the capital gains tax rate is 28 per cent, but President Bush has announced the intention of reducing it to half that level. In a statement justifying that plan it was pointed out that only the UK and Australia tax entrepreneurs' gains more highly than the USA. Annex II (below, pp.26-27) gives more details about the conditions under which the countries concerned allow entrepreneurs to receive their capital gains tax free. It is clear that many countries, often with governments whose politics are generally well to the left of our own, recognise the vital importance of encouraging enterprise and the importance of capital gains tax concessions in this context.

Table 2

CAPITAL GAINS TAX FOR ENTREPRENEURS

Tax Rate on Long-Term Holdings of Less Than 25% of the Equity of the Company, 1989

FRANCE	Nil
GERMANY	Nil
ITALY	Nil
HOLLAND	Nil
USA	28%
UK	40%

Source: Arthur Andersen Study for BVCA.

British entrepreneurs will probably set up their first business in the UK. For their second, when they have the financial independence to choose where to live, capital gains tax differentials often become an important deciding factor. Any venture capitalist will tell you about successful UK entrepreneurs whose second business is in the USA or France or Germany. Capital gains tax drives business offshore.

5. Shortage of Seed Capital Caused by Taxation

So much for the shortage of management for small companies in the UK. What of the shortage of money? In the USA the venture capital industry provides some $4 billion of capital for private companies each year, against some $60 billion from private individuals.

In the UK it is almost impossible to raise seed capital – the first £25,000 to £200,000 of capital for a business. Professional venture capitalists find it too expensive to manage this size of investment, though the BVCA is trying to encourage the setting up of seed funds. Wealthier individuals choose not to invest their money in this way. Economists often argue that it is right to tax capital gains from risky investments, such as small companies, at the same rates as those from safe investments, such as second homes, because the market will magically equalise the after-tax rates of return. This argument is fundamentally flawed, because most investors cannot invest in enough small companies to achieve the diversification of risk necessary to equalise the rates of return. More importantly, what we are concerned with is the real behaviour of individuals rather than economic theories. In fact, the

British investing public rejects the arguments of the economists and plumps for second homes every time. The solution to this problem is not to send the British investing public back to college; it is to cut capital gains tax on unquoted companies.

We have argued that high rates of capital gains tax on unquoted companies seriously deter the flow of management and money into those companies and that this is bad for the economy. Every major European country accepts this and adjusts its tax régime accordingly. Why not the British?

6. The Paradox of Government Policy

It is paradoxical that the Government has acknowledged the problem and the fact that capital gains tax is the key to its solution. The Business Expansion Scheme (BES) was set up to help overcome the financial side of the problem. Unfortunately, however, the scheme prohibits management from making BES investments in companies for which they work. Managers with cash to spare can make CGT-free investments in their homes, in their pension funds, in classic cars and in their friends' businesses. But if they want to leave the safety of a big company and invest in their own business, then capital gains tax they must pay. The justification for this is sometimes said to be the fear that if managers could gain CGT exemption through the BES in companies they set up themselves, they might be able to switch income to capital gains, thus saving themselves 40 per cent tax. But, given the existence of corporation tax and advance corporation tax, it is very hard to see how this could be done in practice. Certainly the principal industrial countries on the continent of Europe find themselves able to live with the problem.

Curiously enough, in the 1970s managers in the UK could in theory have done what the Revenue fears and exchanged 98 per cent income tax for 30 per cent capital gains tax, a 68 per cent saving. For all that time it was clearly not the government's assessment that this was an insuperable problem. So it is hard to believe that this can be a real barrier to allowing entrepreneurs BES-style capital gains tax relief in their own companies, when the margin of advantage has fallen from 68 to zero per cent.

Personal Equity Plans (PEPs) are another indication that the Government accepts that capital gains tax rates affect investment decisions. Yet here unquoted companies are specifically excluded. It is argued that this is to prevent people peddling doubtful unquoted shares. This argument certainly cannot be used to justify preventing managers from making PEP investments in unquoted companies for which they work. This modest amendment to PEPs would certainly help with the management problem, though a more attractive change would be to allow anyone to make PEP investments in unquoted companies. If the PEP investment limit were to be raised, either solely for management or for all investments in unquoted companies, a major improvement would result.

Given that the Government seems to accept that cutting capital gains tax would encourage the development of new businesses, what reasons might be adduced for not abolishing capital gains tax on unquoted companies, or for not adopting one of the lesser initiatives described above? The Government might at one time have felt that enterprise was alive and well and needed no further encouragement. This is a less tenable position today. Encouraging new companies that will export their products, or produce products that will substitute for imports, must benefit the economy. Perhaps there is some overwhelming practical or philosophical justification for making the CGT rate on unquoted companies the same as the income tax rate? If so, the justification cannot be revenue generation. It is now difficult to deny that CGT revenue is maximised at a rate well below 40 per cent.[1] Apart from implications for the revenue, there is the damage to the economy of managements failing to sell out when they should (for strategic or management reasons) because of a desire to avoid capital gains tax.

7. Revenue Gains from Abolishing Capital Gains Tax

If the fear of loss of revenue from capital gains tax concessions is a factor influencing Treasury thinking, the notional losses should be weighed against the increased revenue resulting from the higher profits and greater wage payments and other forms of additional economic activity that would flow from the introduction of better management into small companies. This is difficult to assess; but an attempt is made in Annex III (below, pp.28-29), which is based on the MORI survey mentioned above. The starting point of the calculation is the assumption that for a capital gain of, say, five times the original investment to be achieved, the profitability of the company must have been enhanced by a similar ratio. This would usually imply an increase in sales and in employment. In the example shown, the corporation and income tax gains over a five-year period are more than seven times the capital gains tax that would

---

[1] See Chapter 4, below, pp.53-57.

be forgone if the entrepreneur paid no capital gains tax. And, of course, the corporation and income tax gains continue in succeeding years. While the figures used in the example are only illustrative, they show that the corporation and income tax revenues from a growing business are much more important than the capital gains tax revenue arising from the sale of the entrepreneur's stake. So, if exempting entrepreneurs from capital gains tax were to have even a modest impact on the number of skilled managers starting or joining new companies, the revenue consequences would be positive. This broader view of the impact of selective capital gains tax concessions has no doubt played its part in establishing other countries' more enlightened approach to the issue.

8. Gains on Unquoted Shares not Analogous to Income

The argument that capital gains and income from investment are essentially the same and should be taxed accordingly is much disputed and is, in any case, irrelevant for those who believe that tax policy should be based on its economic effects rather than on tax philosophy. However, we do not accept the philosophical argument since there are many different types of capital gain, some of which may be regarded as forms of income, while others cannot. In the former category, an investment in a large, blue-chip quoted company may generate both income and capital gains. The balance between the two will vary for a number of reasons, including the company's dividend policy, but it is arguable that the receipts are of the same nature. However, the capital gain that may or may not accrue from investing in a small unquoted company is clearly not the same as the income generated from investing the same amount of money in a building society account or indeed a blue-chip equity. The differentiating factors are the risks involved and the illiquidity of the investment in the unquoted company. The argument that capital gains are a form of income may have gained currency only because those putting it forward have never seriously contemplated making an investment in an unquoted company. Be that as it may, it is notable that those arguing for the taxation of capital gains as though they were income temper their approach with reality in that they stop short of allowing capital losses against income tax. For similar practical reasons, they should also recognise that in the UK people need encouragement to make high-risk decisions with their careers or with their money. The most effective way of encouraging these economically desirable decisions is through capital gains tax concessions.

9. Recommendations

From the venture capital perspective, one of the most effective and least expensive ways for the Government to promote small companies would be to reduce or eliminate capital gains tax on gains made by all investors in such companies. As a less significant alternative, gains made by managers on the shares of the unquoted companies that employ them should be exempt from capital gains tax. Extending PEPs to cover shares in all unquoted companies or at least the shares owned by managers of an unquoted company would confer benefits on the economy. The removal of the present age limits for retirement relief from capital gains tax and an increase in the amounts available for relief (both measures building on precedents in the Finance Act 1991) would extend a lower or zero rate of capital gains tax to a wider range of entrepreneurs. This would be particularly valuable if the minimum shareholding level qualifying for retirement relief was abolished or sharply reduced from the current level of 25 per cent. More radically, a seven-year taper to zero, on the analogy of the present régime for inheritance tax, has the particular merit of counteracting short-termism and a general logic extending beyond entrepreneurs to all holders of unquoted company shares and indeed to holders of all assets chargeable to capital gains tax.

ANNEX I

Tax and the Manager/Entrepreneur

○ 50% PAY CUT

— from £60,000 to £30,000

○ 5% OF THE EQUITY

	1979	1991
Income tax rate	83%	40%
Capital gains tax rate	30%	40%
Lost income (after tax) p.a.	£5, 100	£18,000
Value in 5 years (invested at 9% net)	£33,000	£117,000
Capital gain to break-even		
— after tax	£33,000	£117,000
— before tax	£47,000	£195,000
— company value	£942,000	£3.9m.
Capital gain = 4 x lost income		
— after tax	£132,000	£468,000
— before tax	£188,000	£780,000
— company value	£3.76m.	£15.6m.

ANNEX II
Summary of Taxation Treatment by Country: Selected Countries

	UK	*France*	*Germany*
Immediate tax deduction for cost of investment	No	Minimal credit only	No
Interest relief on funds borrowed by entrepreneur to make the investment	Maybe	Yes, up to FF100,000 or 50% of salary	Yes
Tax on sale of entrepreneur's shares	40% after indexation	17% but if shareholding is less than 25% of any unquoted company then gain is tax free.	If shares held for more than 6 months and represent less than 25% of company then gain is tax free. If shares held for less than 6 months then full income tax rates apply. Otherwise gains taxed at half normal income tax rate.
Wealth tax	None	May apply if assets worth over FF4m at rates to 1·1%.	Up to 0·5%
Gift/inheritance tax	Rates up to 40% with reductions for significant holdings.	Rates to 40%	Rates to 20%
Income tax rates	Up to 40%	Up to 56·8%	Up to 56% (53% from 1990)

Note: Above information shows tax treatment of an entrepreneur who invests equity capital in a company which fully employs him.

...ain	Italy	Holland	USA	Ireland
...)	No	No	No	BES relief
...) to ...00	No	Yes	Yes subject to active participation.	Yes subject to certain conditions.
...ain taxed ...income ...x rates up ...56%. ...pering ...ief and ...dexation ...ply.	If shares are a minority interest (as deemed) or are held for more than 5 years then gain is tax free.	20% if he and close relatives have substantial holdings (greater than one-third; otherwise nil).	Gain taxed at income tax rates. No indexation.	Between 30% and 60% depending on period of ownership. Indexation applies.
...p to 2%	None	Up to 0·8%	None	None
...ates to ...6%	Rates to 31%	Rates to 68%	Rates to 55%	Rates up to 55%
...p to 56%	Up to 50%	Up to 72% (reducing to 60% in 1990)	Rates of 15% and 28% but marginal 33% rate for income between $71,900 and $149,250.	Up to 56%

ANNEX III
Tax Revenue from Growing Companies

1. ASSUMPTIONS
   - Entrepreneur invests £40k in year 1 and realises in year 5 at 5 × money, i.e. £200k.
   - Year 1 profits of company are £160k pre-tax, rising to £480k by year 5 in even steps of £80k p.a.
   - Tax rates: capital gains – 40%
     Marginal corporation tax – 33%.
   - Additional 6 employees join each year, at average salary of £15,000 p.a.
   - Incremental purchases made amount to 30% of turnover.

2. Capital Gains Tax forgone (assuming scheme exists)
   40% × (£200k – £40k) = £64k in year 5.

3. Corporation Tax gained—based on incremental profits beyond level existing when investment made (assuming entrepreneur is responsible for these incremental profits).

	Yr 1	*Yr 2*	*Yr 3*	*Yr 4*	*Yr 5*
Total PBT*	160	240	320	400	480
Incremental PBT	–	80	160	240	320
Incremental Tax	–	26	53	79	106

TOTAL INCREMENTAL TAX = £264K

* Profit before tax.

NB: As company falls within band for the small companies rate (i.e. PBT of £100k-£1 million), the actual marginal rate is 35%. However, to prevent the assumptions about the absolute level of profitability distorting the calculation, the normal and more conservative marginal rate of 33% has been used.

4. Additional Corporation Tax gained—based on the fact that this company's purchases will represent additional sales for other companies. Purchases for the invested company amount to 30% of turnover, and assuming that the suppliers have a similar cost structure, the additional PBT in the suppliers would be 30% as follows:

	Yr 1	*Yr 2*	*Yr 3*	*Yr 4*	*Yr 5*
Additional PBT	–	24	48	72	96
Additional Tax	–	8	16	24	32

TOTAL ADDITIONAL TAX = £79K

5. PAYE generated as follows:

	Yr 1	Yr 2	Yr 3	Yr 4	Yr 5
Total incremental employees	–	6	12	18	24
Incremental PAYE	–	15	30	45	60

TOTAL INCREMENTAL INCOME TAX = £150K

* Based on full married man's allowance of £5,165, tax at 25% is £2,458. If a single person's allowance is used, tax would be £2,888. For illustrative purposes, £2,500 of income tax per person is used.

6. The multiplier effects do not stop here. Each of the suppliers would themselves make purchases, adding further to Corporation tax payable. Each of the additional employees would spend this income, creating more revenue and more jobs. However, quantification beyond the first levels of 'domino' effects becomes very difficult and has not been attempted here.

7. To summarise, the corporation and income tax gains are £493,000, nearly seven times as much as the £64,000 of capital gains tax forgone.

3

CAPITAL GAINS TAX IN OECD COUNTRIES[1]

Cedric Sandford
Professor Emeritus of Political Economy,
University of Bath

1. Introduction

INTERNATIONAL COMPARISONS of particular taxes invariably reveal marked differences amongst countries, reflecting their individual histories, social and economic structure and national philosophies, as well as the *ad hoc* way in which hard-pressed governments have responded to the exigencies of the moment. These reasons for diversity are all apparent with capital gains tax (CGT); but added to them is a further reason for difference: a lack of agreement on the basic nature of the tax.

All countries tax to income tax some kinds of disposals which can be construed as generating capital gains. Thus assets purchased for resale generate a gain charged to income tax or corporation tax where the transactions are part of regular business activities – even if they would not be so treated in other circumstances. Perhaps the only other feature common to all countries is that when gains are taxed, they are taxed when they are realised, not as they accrue.

---

[1] The author was responsible for preparing a report for the OECD on the basis of information supplied by its Members. After revisions in the light of discussions in a Working Party of the Committee on Fiscal Affairs, the report was published as *Taxation of Net Wealth, Capital Transfers and Capital Gains of Individuals,* Paris: OECD, 1988. This chapter draws heavily on that report to which reference should be made for further details. The author acknowledges, with thanks, permission to reproduce from that report.

Some countries regard *any* capital gains as essentially equivalent to income; whilst to others 'short-term' or 'speculative' gains by individuals are seen as income-equivalent whilst 'longer-term' gains are not. In yet other countries capital gains are seen as a suitable object for a tax separate from income tax.

Even where the capital gains of individuals are seen as equivalent to income, few countries tax them precisely as other forms of income, because of the particular need to exclude purely monetary gains, for *de minimis* administrative reasons, or for other considerations. Where capital gains are included within the income tax code, it is common for a proportion only of the gain to be treated as income – that proportion being arbitrarily determined. Where countries distinguish short- from longer-term gains there is similarly an arbitrariness about the dividing line, with different countries drawing it in different places.

Another distinction which creeps into some capital gains taxes, and adds complication and flouts principle, is to accord different treatment to different classes of assets, in particular movable and immovable property.

International Comparisons – 'Broad Distinction' Only

As a consequence of these varied treatments, no simple classification of countries, such as those with and those without capital gains taxes, is meaningful. Table 1 makes a broad distinction between countries which impose a separate tax on the capital gains of individuals and those which use the income tax code. Amongst the latter an attempt is made to distinguish the degree of comprehensiveness of the tax. Broadly speaking, countries with 'no special provisions' tax capital gains only if they are of the nature of business receipts. The classification is necessarily somewhat arbitrary. In particular, the distinction between a country with a separate capital gains tax and one listed under income tax with comprehensive coverage is often one of form rather than substance. Thus Australia and the United States (from 1987) subject capital gains to full income tax rates on a wide base whilst most of the other countries in that category subject gains to a very different regime from ordinary income. Similarly, the base and rates of those countries with a separate capital gains tax vary substantially from each other and any particular country may, in effect, provide a capital gains tax regime nearer to that of countries in the income tax categories than others with separate gains taxes. To take an extreme example, since 1988, although capital gains tax in the United Kingdom is a separate tax, capital gains have been subject to income tax rates (though with separate thresholds).

Table 1:

Main Methods of Taxing the Capital Gains of Private Persons as at November 1987

Separate Tax on Capital Gains	Income Tax		
	Comprehensive coverage with provisions including long-term capital gains	Special provisions mainly restricted to short-term or speculative gains	No special provisions
Denmark Ireland Portugal Switzerland (Zurich)[1] United Kingdom[2]	Australia Canada Finland France Japan[3] Luxembourg Norway Spain[4] Sweden United States	Austria Belgium Germany Turkey	Greece Italy[5] Netherlands New Zealand[6]

Source: OECD, *Taxation of Net Wealth . . ., op. cit.*

[1] Capital gains on private property are taxed by the cantons and not the Confederation; all cantons impose CGT on immovable property, in most cases as a tax separate from income tax.

[2] As from 1988 the rates of CGT were equated with the taxpayer's top marginal rate of income tax.

[3] In 1989 CGT on sales of stock by individuals was made general whereas previously there had been wide exemption provisions.

[4] Also a separate CGT at local level on gains from urban immovable property.

[5] Provisions have been enacted for a CGT on disposal of shares, bonds and similar investments as from 1991.

[6] Early in 1990 the New Zealand government issued a consultative document proposing a comprehensive taxation of capital gains to income tax; however, this approach was modified soon afterwards in favour of a more limited look at ways of reducing anomalies. The proposal to introduce a capital gains tax was abandoned by the incoming government after the general election in 1990.

Some of these differences are explored in the remainder of this paper, the purpose of which is to provide a comparative perspective on capital gains taxes by describing practice in a range of countries, rather than to advance any normative views.

The data in the main text of the OECD report[2] related to the position at 1 April 1986, with some reference to changes known to be in train; an Appendix to the report listed changes between 1 April 1986 and November 1987. This paper incorporates these changes in the text and tables, which therefore refer to the position at November 1987 to ensure comparability. Changes of significance known to have taken place since then are also referred to in the text and added by way of footnotes to the tables.

In a short paper it is necessary to be highly selective about the issues to be covered in more detail. The following have been chosen as of general significance: the objectives of capital gains taxes; treatment of short- and long-term gains; treatment of losses; rates and thresholds; revenue considerations; treatment of death and gifts; and treatment of the principal private residence.

2. Why Countries Adopted Capital Gains Tax

In response to an OECD questionnaire, the main reason given by countries for adopting a capital gains tax was what was usually described as 'fiscal equity': such gains constituted an accretion of economic or spending power and horizontal equity required that it be taken into the tax reckoning. Widening the tax base, limiting income tax avoidance, improving vertical equity, were other reasons given, and France saw it as a way of providing additional data on capital ownership to check avoidance and evasion of inheritance tax and gift duties. Australia also saw a capital gains tax as an instrument for reducing investment distortion, which, in the absence of a gains tax, went disproportionately towards assets generating capital growth rather than income.

One country, the Netherlands, which had recently debated the issue in Parliament, had rejected a comprehensive capital gains tax because of high administrative costs in relation to revenue, technical complications, and bad economic and financial effects.

3. Short- and Long-Term Gains

Some countries, including Germany and Austria, tax only short-term gains; in others both short- and long-term gains are taxed but the tax on

---

[2] See note 1, above, p.31.

long-term gains is less heavy; yet other countries tax both kinds of gain without distinction.

In Germany, gains are taxed as income if realised within six months of acquisition if movables, or two years if immovables; in Austria the corresponding periods are one year and five years.

Countries which tax both long- and short-term gains may differentiate between them in one of several ways. They may charge long-term gains at a lower rate than short-term; often, as in Finland and Denmark, they charge short-term gains to full income tax rates, but apply lower rates to long-term gains. They may, as in Sweden and France, differentiate by applying the same rate to both, but on only a proportion of the long-term gain. Another method, adopted by Australia, is to apply the same rate of tax to both, in this case the rate of income tax, but to index only the gains held for over a year.

Differentiation according to the period of gain may take the form of more elaborate, tapering rates. Thus Ireland taxes gains realised in under a year at 50 per cent, since April 1990 (previously 60 per cent); but the rate diminishes in three stages, to 30 per cent, which is charged on assets held over six years.

Still other countries take no account of differences in the length of time between acquisition and disposal; thus, the United States (since 1987) charges all gains to full income tax and Canada charges the same proportion of the gain to income tax, irrespective of the period of accrual.

The history of the UK capital gains tax is instructive. Capital gains tax was first applied to short-term gains only, in 1962. A comprehensive capital gains tax was introduced in 1965 which distinguished between the two, taxing gains of under a year at full income tax rates and other gains at a flat rate. This distinction was abolished in 1971 when all chargeable gains were made subject to the flat rate. Then, in 1988, the rates for both, without distinction, were aligned to the individual's top marginal rate of income tax.

The Arguments for Differentiation

Various arguments have been used to justify differentiation. If capital gains are treated as income it is appropriate to subject short-term gains to income tax; but to treat gains which have accrued over many years as income in the year of disposal would appear unduly harsh if income tax is progressive. However, this argument for differentiation loses much of its force if income tax rates are low; thus the change in United States practice derives from the 1986 Tax Reform Act, which slashed income tax rates. Another argument for having a tax rate decreasing with the length of holding is to compensate, in a rough and ready way, for the inflationary element in the gain. Indexation of the acquisition price may be held to be a better way of achieving this objective; but as different kinds of asset appreciate at different rates, it falls short of full equity for taxpayers and is less simple than rate differentiation.

In countries which do not consider capital gains to be income, the case for taxing short-term gains more heavily than long-term, or taxing short-term gains only, rests on the consideration that short-term gains are rather like business gains and, if not income, have similar characteristics; they are 'speculative' gains, entered into for a quick profit, rather than as a long-term investment.

In the UK the abolition of the distinction between short- and long-term gains rested on practical considerations. As far as possible, in order to reduce tax rates, taxpayers abstained from realising short-term gains; thus the short-term tax produced little revenue to justify the additional administrative complication of separate legal provisions. Moreover, the arbitrary dividing line created inequity between taxpayers whose disposals came just before it as against just afterwards.

4. Treatment of Losses

In arriving at the tax base, as a general rule countries allow losses to be offset against gains. Occasionally a loss offset may be restricted to the same class of asset; France allows losses only in respect of securities and such losses can be set only against gains from securities.

In the extent to which losses can be carried backward or forward there is considerable difference between countries. For instance, Germany, which taxes only short-term gains, allows losses to be set against gains only in the year in which they occur. Similarly in Finland, short-term losses can be offset only against short-term gains and then only in the year in which they occur; and long-term losses are not deductible at all. Ireland allows excess losses to be carried forward indefinitely, but not backward, save to a limited extent in the case of death.

Where countries subject gains to income tax, especially where full income tax rates apply, it is more logical to allow capital losses to be deductible against ordinary income than where a separate capital gains tax exists; but treatment varies. In Norway, apart from gains and losses on shares (which are taxed at a flat 30 per cent and where losses are deductible only against gains from shares), losses can be set against ordinary income and can be carried forward 10 years. Spain, which (until 1991) taxed both short- and long-term gains to ordinary income tax rates, allowed losses to be offset only against gains but allowed them to be carried forward indefinitely. Australia, although taxing gains at income tax rates, allows losses to be set only against taxable gains (and losses on listed personal-use assets can be set only against gains on personal-use assets); but excess losses can be carried forward, unindexed, indefinitely.

Where the married couple or the family is the tax unit, most countries allow the losses of one spouse to be offset against the gains of another, though Finland is an exception. Such transfers are not possible where spouses have opted for separate assessment or where the tax unit is the individual.

Several countries, notably France, Spain and Australia, have averaging provisions, to prevent a progressive tax applying too harshly in the year of realisation of gains.

5. Rates and Thresholds

The rates and thresholds of capital gains tax as at November 1987 are set out in Tables 2a and 2b, for countries with separate capital gains taxes and those where gains are comprehensively taxed under the income tax code. Changes of substance known to have taken place since November 1987 – the latest date for which information is recorded in the OECD study – are listed in the comment column.

6. Revenue Yield

Where countries tax capital gains under the income tax code they often cannot give separate figures for the yield of capital gains taxation. Where such information can be provided, it is clear that the direct yield, both as a percentage of tax revenue and of GDP, is generally small. It is also a more fluctuating revenue than that of most other taxes; in a time of stock exchange or property boom, for example, it may rise considerably, but fall at a time of slump. It is important to realise, however, that the addition to revenue from the existence of a capital gains tax may be more than the direct yield of the tax. One object of a capital gains tax is to prevent investment distortion by investors seeking to avoid income tax who therefore acquired assets yielding capital gain but little or no income. In so far as a capital gains tax checks such distortion, it increases the yield from income tax.

Table 2a: **Rates and Thresholds, November 1987**
(a) Countries with Separate Capital Gains Tax

Country	Rate of tax		General threshold per annum	Comments and recent changes
	Long–term gains	Short–term gains		
Denmark	50%	As long–term	No general threshold	
Ireland	Assets owned between % 1 and 3 years 50 2 and 6 years 35 over 6 years 30	60%[1] (gains realised within one year)	Ir£2,000 (£1,780) (double for married couple)	[1]With effect from April 1990, this rate was reduced to 50%. No formal distinction between short–term and long–term but a tapering rate
Portugal	12% or 24%	As long–term	–	24% rate applies to sale of building land
Switzerland (Zurich)	Progressive scale 10–40%	As long–term (but see comment)	In general SF 2,000 (£815)	Additional charge on immovable property held under 2 years; reduction on immovable property held over 5 years
United Kingdom	30%	As long–term	£6,600[2]	[2]As from 1988, the rates of CGT were aligned with the taxpayer's top marginal rate of income tax. In 1991 in the context of individual taxation of income, the CGT threshold was £5,500; this was increased to £5,800 in 1992

Table 2b: Rates and Thresholds, November 1987
(b) Countries with Comprehensive Coverage within Income Tax

Country	Rate of tax		General threshold per annum	Comments and recent changes
	Long-term gains	Short-term gains		
Australia	Real gain taxed as income	Taxed as income	No special exemption	Five-year averaging provisions.
Canada	Half gain taxed as income[1]	As long-term	Lifetime exemption of C$100,000 (£42,797)	Higher exemption for farm property and, from 1988, shares in small business corporations. From February 1992, active business requirement for exemption of real estate. [1]This proportion increased to ⅔ for 1988 and ¾ for 1990.
Finland	20% of gain over Mk 1 million (£136,000) taxed as income	As investment income	Long-term gains only (as indicated)	16% tax on capital gains from the alienation of unquoted company shares from September 1990.
France	Rates depend on nature of asset and period held	Personal property held for 1 year or less and real property for two years or less taxed as ordinary income	FF 6,000 (£592); but higher thresholds for different classes of asset	As of 1 January 1991, the tax on land and buildings has been subjected to an extended taper so that total exemption takes place after 32 years instead of, as hitherto, 22 years.

Table 2b: **Rates and Thresholds, November 1987**
(contd.) **(b) Countries with Comprehensive Coverage within Income Tax**

Country	Rate of tax		General threshold per annum	Comments and recent changes
	Long-term gains	Short-term gains		
Japan	Half gain is taxed as income except for land and buildings to which a special rate applies	As income tax but special rate on land and buildings	Y 500,000 (£2,080)	Short-term gains defined as under 5 years. New tax regime for stock transactions (previously widely exempted for individuals) introduced April 1989. The special rate of long-term CGT on land and buildings increased from 20 to 30 per cent as from 1 April 1991.
Luxembourg	Half income tax rates. In general long-term tax applies only to property	As income tax	LF 1,250,000 (£20,010) (over 10-year period)	Exemption of capital gains from the disposal of substantial participations, from 1991.
Norway	As income tax, except gains from land may be taxed at 30%, taxpayer's option	As long-term, except gains from shares taxed at 30% (exempt if held over 2 years)	No special exemption	

Country	Rate of tax		General threshold per annum	Comments and recent changes
	Long-term gains	Short-term gains		
Spain	As income tax (except for lower rate for transfers by gift and at death)	As long-term	No special exemption	Averaging provisions relating to number of years held. In 1989 rate on transfers by gift and death increased from 8% to 20%. In 1990 a wide range of exemptions was introduced for long-term capital gains, including capital gains at death. An annual exemption of 500,000 pesetas (£2,700) was made effective from January 1991 and short-term gains (1 year or less) became taxable as ordinary income.
Sweden	A proportion of the gain is taxed as income, the proportion depending on the nature of the property and the period held, eg. 40% on shares held 2 years or longer[1]	As income tax	No general threshold	[1]From 1990 taxable part of gains from shares held 2 years or longer increased to 50%.
United States	As income tax	As income tax	No special exemption	

7. Treatment of Gains at Death and on Gifts

At the death of the owner of assets on which capital gains tax liability has accrued there are three possible treatments, all of which are found in OECD countries:

1. The time of death may be deemed a realisation and tax charged as if the deceased had actually disposed of the asset. This is the treatment in Canada and (formerly) in Spain, but with some exceptions; for example, in Canada liability is deferred in respect of assets passing to a surviving spouse.

2. Liability may be deferred until the gains are actually realised by the persons who succeed to the ownership of the assets, where the tax is payable on the whole of the gain since the deceased acquired it. Deferred liability is the general rule in Australia, Denmark, Japan, Luxembourg and Sweden.

3. Exemption may be granted at death; the successor is then treated as having acquired the asset at its market value at the date of death. This practice is followed in the majority of countries.

Exemption at death can be objected to on grounds both of equity and of efficiency. It seems unfair that, where two persons have gains of the same amount, the one who realises the gains pays tax, even if he dies the day after realisation, whilst the other, who holds the assets till death, escapes tax. Further, exemption creates a locking-in effect through owners clinging to assets they would otherwise have sold, thereby reducing the mobility of capital. On the other hand, since in most cases a charge to capital gains tax at death coincides with the imposition of death duties, a double charge may be considered excessive.

There is also a possible difficulty with deferred liability. In effecting the dispositions from an estate, in principle an executor needs to take account of deferred liability associated with any assets which are transferred to a beneficiary (instead of money) in satisfaction of an amount due to him from the estate.

The same three treatments are found with lifetime gifts; but rather more countries treat lifetime gifts as an occasion for charge to capital gains tax and two countries treat capital gains tax on lifetime gifts as a deferred liability whilst exempting transfers at death. The reason for this less favourable treatment of gifts by several countries is, presumably, that a gift is a voluntary act at the time of the taxpayer's choosing, whereas the time of transfer at death is not within his control.

Almost all countries exempt the gain where the donee is a charity.

8. Exemption and Reliefs: the Principal Private Residence

All countries offer exemption or reliefs for some classes of asset, mainly on social and economic grounds or for reasons of practical administration. The proceeds of life insurance policies and superannuation schemes are frequently exempt (though they may attract income tax). Gains on government and other bonds and on small savings schemes may be exempt. There is a wide range of reliefs for gains on chattels. There are frequently exemptions or reliefs for productive assets.

Gains from the disposal of a principal private residence are almost invariably exempt or accorded substantial relief. Conditions are often imposed to ensure that the residence has been the taxpayer's principal private residence, and in the United Kingdom, Ireland and Australia, where the residence has been occupied by the taxpayer for only part of the period of ownership, only part of the gain is exempt. In Denmark exemption only applies to smaller properties and in Japan only to the first tranche of the gain. In a number of countries, for instance, Spain, the United States and Sweden, relief is, in general, conditional on the purchase of another residence within a specified time-limit and may be restricted where the new residence costs more than the sale price of the old.

4

EMPIRICAL SUPPORT FOR REDUCING RATES OF CAPITAL GAINS TAX IN THE UNITED STATES

Ronald Utt

1. Introduction

HOW TO TAX CAPITAL GAINS remains one of the most controversial issues confronting economic policy-makers. Though a number of countries, like the Republic of Korea, do not tax capital gains at all, the United States approach has been a roller coaster. In the mid-1970s, for example, capital gains were taxed as high as 35 per cent; this top rate was cut to 28 per cent in 1978 and cut further to 20 per cent by the 1981 Reagan tax reduction. Then the pendulum swung abruptly, and surprisingly, back in the comprehensive overhaul of the tax code in 1986. As a result, capital gains today are taxed at the same rate as ordinary income. This rightly alarms many economists, because a high capital gains tax discourages investment, savings and entrepreneurial risk-taking. Without these, the USA will become internationally less competitive.

2. Current Prospects for a Cut in the Rate of Capital Gains Tax

Notwithstanding repeated and intense efforts to restore the preferential tax treatment for capital gains relatively to income, the situation remains much as it has been since 1986, when the Tax Reform Act of 1986 overturned three-quarters of a century of US tax policy by treating capital gains as ordinary income for tax purposes.

President Bush entered office in early 1989 with the commitment to restore the preference as an integral part of his agenda. Despite the efforts of his opponents to define the issue as one of 'fairness' and attempt to pit the rich against the not-so-rich, President Bush's proposal to lower the capital gains tax garnered considerable middle-class support. As a consequence, and over the harsh objections of their leadership, scores of Democratic Congressmen in the House of Representatives crossed over and voted in favour of a reduction in the capital gains tax. The legislation received the necessary majority and was subsequently sent to the Senate for approval.

In the Senate the opposition regrouped and through parliamentary manoeuvring was able to create significant procedural obstacles that could not be overcome. The opponents were successful and Congress adjourned for the session without enacting the legislation. As a result of delaying the decision until the next session of Congress, the considerable momentum of public support behind the legislation was dissipated during the interval. When Congress did reconvene, opponents quickly recognised the decline in support and used this as an opportunity to defeat the bill.

Worsening Budget Deficit

The initiative was unable to recover from this setback and the probability of enactment is now significantly below that of 1989. In part, this reflects a simple loss of political momentum. Additionally, the decline in support also reflects a worsening of the Federal government's budget deficit. Although there is no evidence to support the commonly held notion that there would be a loss of revenue from a capital gains rate reduction, intuitive plausibility induces most Americans to believe otherwise, and this leads to a further lessening of support for a rate cut as annual budget deficits rise above $300 billion dollars.

At the same time, with the Bush Administration continuing to move to the centre and embrace 'pragmatic and realistic' policies, the proposal to reduce the capital gains tax rate appears increasingly inconsistent with the overall tenor of the administration. As a consequence, Congress and the media question the President's sincerity and view his continued advocacy of the rate cut as nothing more than a perfunctory attempt to honour a commitment to the more conservative wing of the party.

For these reasons, it is unlikely that a capital gains tax rate reduction will occur during the next five years unless it becomes an integral part of a comprehensive economic growth programme endorsed by the new Administration in early 1993, following the 1992 Presidential elections.

3. Opposition to Lower Rates of Capital Gains Tax

The prospect of reductions in the rates of capital gains tax has generated intense opposition from a variety of sources - notably organised labour. Opponents of capital gains tax rate reductions attempt to build their case on three arguments:

1. **Equity and fairness:** Capital gains preferences, critics say, favour the wealthy by providing a disproportionate share of the benefits to upper income taxpayers.

2. **Cost:** A capital gains tax rate reduction is said to increase the federal deficit because it will reduce tax revenues.

3. **Effectiveness:** A lower capital gains tax rate, critics argue, will have little effect on the decisions of individuals to invest or engage in entrepreneurial activity.

Each of these criticisms is challenged by supporters of capital gains tax reductions. They marshal an extensive collection of facts and research to demonstrate that the opponents' positions are either exaggerated or simply untrue.

1. *Equity and fairness*: The evidence indicates that the concern about fairness is misplaced. When income is properly measured, the data reveal that capital gains realisations are spread rather evenly throughout different income levels and do not accrue only to the rich. Indeed, households earning less than $20,000 a year accounted for more than a quarter of all capital gains reported by taxpayers in 1985.

2. *Cost*: Detailed econometric studies of the record since the Second World War indicate that capital gains tax rate cuts actually generate tax revenues by encouraging individuals to invest in taxable assets, unlock realised and taxable gains and redeploy capital efficiently - thus generating taxable income.

3. *Effectiveness*: The two capital gains tax rate increases and the two tax decreases since 1969 provide solid evidence of how individuals, businesses and markets respond to such changes. What the last two decades reveal is that investors, businesses and venture capital markets are sensitive to changes in the capital gains tax rate. The data show that when rates are raised, venture funding slows or

declines; conversely, when the rates are cut, the venture capital market spurts.

Lawmakers considering legislation to reduce taxes on capital gains should examine this evidence carefully. Critics of tax cut proposals level charges that a cut would be bad for the economy and the budget and unfair to moderate and low-income taxpayers. Yet the data refute them, suggesting strongly that a cut would boost the economy while spreading tax benefits to all major income groups.

In the absence of appropriate tax exclusions, the gauntlet of taxation faced by investors discriminates against capital income, discourages savings and investment and harms US international competitiveness by raising the cost of capital for Americans relatively to that of foreign competitors, many of whose countries fully exempt capital gains from income taxes.[1]

4. The Impact of Capital Taxation on Investment Decisions

Advocates of a reduced tax rate or an exclusion for capital gains contend that these changes would increase savings and investment by decreasing the cost of capital to a firm and increasing the return on investment to the investor. At present, the gauntlet of corporate income taxes, the taxation of capital gains and personal income taxes creates a large gap between what business earns on an investment and what the individual shareholders ultimately receive. This gap is often referred to as the 'tax wedge'. Reduced tax rates would encourage individuals to acquire financial assets by raising the after-tax rate of return. Such rate reductions would make investments in new and growing firms relatively attractive because most benefits of such investments would be in the form of capital appreciation rather than income paid in taxable dividends.

For the firm, a lower capital gains tax rate would reduce the effective cost of capital and encourage the acquisition of productive assets. For the new and growing firm, with limited income but unlimited promise, a lower rate or capital gains exclusion would encourage investors to take risks by offering the opportunity for a potentially higher reward.

What the Data Reveal

Several studies and surveys on the effect of capital gains tax rates on the willingness of investors to acquire shares in new firms support the view

---

[1] See Chapter 3 (above, pp.31-43).

that rate reductions have stimulated venture capital market growth. Although some analysts challenge this contention, arguing that a substantial portion of venture funding comes from non-taxed sources such as pension funds, the surveys and studies do not support this view and instead indicate that the individual investor is an important participant in the venture capital market.

In a 1988 study by economists John Freear of the University of New Hampshire and William Wetzel of Babson College, questionnaires were sent to the chief executive officers of 1,073 technology-based ventures founded in New England between 1975 and 1986.[2] The results from the 284 firms responding indicate:

○ More new technology-based firms raise equity-type capital from private individuals than from any other outside source, including venture capital firms.[3]

○ Private individuals are the primary source of outside equity-type capital for new technology-based firms when total funds raised each time the firm goes to the financial market are under $1 million.

○ Private individuals tend to invest earlier in the life of a new technology-based firm than do other outside sources of equity type capital, including venture-type[4] funds.[5]

Dramatic Increase in Capital Raised Through Initial Public Offerings (IPOs)

An analysis of the ebb and flow of venture capital over time indicates that there is a close correlation between the availability of such funds and changes in the capital gains tax rate. Table 1, which presents the trend in Initial Public Offerings (IPOs) as one measure of venture capital

---

[2] John Freear and William E. Wetzel, 'Equity Financing for New Technology-Based Firms', paper prepared for the Babson Entrepreneurship Research Conference, Calgary, Alberta, May 1988.

[3] Equity-type investments are those that provide a share of the ownership to the investor and a right to participate in the profits.

[4] 'Venture-type funds' are professional investment companies that specialise in investing in promising new companies.

[5] The authors' hypothesis that total equity-type capital raised by these firms from private individuals exceeds the total capital raised from other outside sources, including venture capital funds, was not validated by the study. Indeed, the study found that the firms in the sample raised five times more capital from the funds than they did from individuals. Although many of these funds are tax-exempt, many of their investors are not, and the profits and gains of these funds are passed on to the investors who are taxed as individuals or corporations according to whether the earnings were ordinary income or capital gains.

Table 1

**New Capital Raised Through Initial Public Stock Offerings (IPOs):
USA, 1969–1990**

Year	Capital gains tax rate %	Number of IPOs	Dollars raised (billions)
1969	27.50	1,026	2.61
1970	28.91	358	0.78
1971	29.82	391	1.66
1972	30.50	568	2.72
1973	30.91	100	0.33
1974	31.55	15	0.05
1975	31.81	15	0.27
1976	33.49	34	0.23
1977	33.77	40	0.15
1978	34.13	45	0.25
1979	25.97	81	0.51
1980	26.67	237	1.40
1981	24.81	448	3.22
1982	20.00	222	1.45
1983	20.00	884	12.62
1984	20.00	354	3.9
1985	20.00	362	8.6
1986	20.00	719	22.4
1987	28.00	541	24.2
1988	28.00	280	23.4
1989	28.00	241	13.7
1990	28.00	209	10.2

Source: *Going Public: The IPO Reporter* (a publication of IDD, Investment Dealers Digest, Inc., New York) and the US Treasury.

raised in organised securities markets, illustrates the sensitivity of new offerings by firms going public to the capital gains tax rate.[6]

As Table 1 indicates, when rates increased between 1969 and 1978, initial public offerings declined significantly, from an annual average of nearly $2 billion between 1969 and 1972 to an average of just $225 million between 1975 and 1978. But following the major rate reductions in 1979 and again in 1982, the capital raised through IPOs soared, stalling at a plateau beginning in 1986-87 when the rate was raised from 20 per cent to 28 per cent under the 1986 Tax Reform Act. Since then the amount raised has declined.

Table 2 illustrates the same connection between capital formation and capital gains tax rates using figures from the venture capital market.[7] As in the case of IPOs, the venture capital market has expanded when capital gains tax rates are cut and has declined or stagnated when rates are increased.

Opponents of capital gains tax relief argue that such correlations are merely coincidence, not cause and effect. They contend that the growth in the venture capital market really reflects the development and commercialisation of new technologies, or the general improvement in equity markets that occurred during the same period.

Yet such alternative explanations of the correlation are not independent of capital gains tax rates, because changes in capital gains tax rates have a direct influence on these other factors by improving the incentives in the market and encouraging individuals to invest in shares. Lower capital gains tax rates increase the incentive to invest, and this increased demand for assets raises the price of financial assets, such as common stocks. Similarly, when investor interest is increased in securities offering capital gains potential, new and growing firms capable of providing such potential will be encouraged to bring their shares to market. Comparative observations by MIT economist James Poterba in his recent study for the National Bureau of Economic Research offer support for this view. According to Poterba:

'In the decade between 1976 and 1986, the stock of commitments to the US venture capital industry rose at a compound annual rate of 17.1 per cent. Measured in constant dollars, the pool of venture

---

[6] IPOs refer to new capital issued through initial public stock offerings of corporations. This capital flows largely to relatively young rapidly-growing companies.

[7] Venture capital here refers to funds raised by companies that specialise in the shares of new businesses.

Table 2

Supply of Venture Capital Financing: USA, 1969–1990

Year	Net new commitments to venture capital firms	Maximum personal tax rate on capital gains
	$ millions	%
1969	505.7	27.50
1970	271.8	28.91
1971	251.8	29.82
1972	156.9	30.50
1973	133.2	30.91
1974	124.2	31.55
1975	19.8	31.81
1976	93.3	33.49
1977	68.2	33.77
1978	978.1	34.13
1979	449.2	25.97
1980	961.4	26.67
1981	1,627.8	24.81
1982	2,118.6	20.0
1983	5,097.7	20.0
1984	4,590.0	20.0
1985	3,502.3	20.0
1986	3,332.0	20.0
1987	4,184.0	28.0
1988	2,997.0	28.0
1989	2,399.0	28.0
1990	1,847.0	28.0

Source: Column 1, 1969 to 1985: Venture Economics, *Venture Capital Yearbook 1988*, p. 17; 1986 to 1990: *Venture Capital Journal*, March 1991, p. 16. Column 2, US Treasury.

capital funds in 1986 was 4.85 times as large as the pool one decade earlier. In Canada, by comparison, the annual growth rate of venture funds was only 5.7 per cent, so that in 1986 the pool of funds was 1.75 times as large as in 1976. While international comparisons are difficult because of problems in controlling for institutional differences, the finding that venture capital investment grew more rapidly in the United States, the country that reduced its capital gains tax rate, is further supporting evidence for a potential link between capital gains taxation and venture capital.'[8]

Elsewhere in his study, Poterba presents additional information to underscore this relationship.

'Since the Tax Reform Act of 1986, which raised individual capital gains tax rates from 20 per cent to 28 per cent (or in some cases 33 per cent) venture funding has been stable. Total revenue commitments increased six per cent between 1986 and 1987, and preliminary 1988 data suggest that this level has at least been maintained through 1988. The recent growth of venture capital investment in other nations, however, suggests that the post-1986 US performance may reflect a negative effect of tax reform. In the UK, the flow of venture capital commitments nearly doubled between 1986 and 1987. In Canada, venture funding rose even more dramatically, from $209 to $800 million. While the growth of venture capital in Canada and Britain may in part reflect the maturation of their venture capital industries, they provide a useful contrast to the recent US experience.'[9]

5. Consequences for the Tax Revenue of Reducing Rates of Capital Gains Tax

Although the evidence strongly indicates that lower capital gains tax rates encourage individuals to fund risky ventures, many policy-makers still question whether the benefits are worth the potential losses in tax revenues carried by a lower rate of tax on capital gains. Sceptics also believe that a lower rate of taxation bestows disproportionately greater benefits on higher-income individuals than on those with lower incomes.

Proponents of a lower capital gains tax rate counter that, contrary to the intuitively plausible proposition that rate cuts reduce revenues,

---

[8] James M. Poterba, *Venture Capital and Capital Gains Taxation*, New York: National Bureau of Economic Research, Working Paper No. 2832, January 1989, p.17.

[9] *Ibid.*, pp. 2-4.

experience demonstrates just the opposite: every instance of a capital gains tax rate cut has been rapidly followed by a significant increase in capital gains realisations (net capital gains proceeds received from the sale of assets and reported to the Internal Revenue Service) and by higher taxes paid on those gains. By lowering the tax cost of selling assets, and thereby increasing the after-tax yield on such assets relatively to other sources of income and property, lower capital gains tax rates can lead to increased realisations of capital gains and thus to increased tax payments by the owners of those assets.

Lower capital gains tax rates, experience shows, also increase the attractiveness of such assets relatively to other sources of income or profits. This encourages more purchases of such assets, which bids up their prices, leading to higher realisations of capital gains when the assets are sold - both because there are more investors now holding such assets and because the increased demand raises their prices and the profits they generate. Again, this rise in value and volume can mean higher tax payments even at a lower tax rate. And to the extent that such tax rate reductions stimulate more investment, business formation and entrepreneurial activity, then general income tax revenues would also rise.

What the Data Reveal

As Table 3 indicates, the rate cuts of both 1979 and 1982 were followed by large increases in reported capital gains and by increases in capital gains tax payments. Conversely, the tax rate increase enacted in 1969 was followed by declining realisations and lower capital gains tax revenues. Indeed, the $5.9 billion of capital gains revenues received in 1968 was not exceeded until 1976. The high rate of revenue in 1986 was largely due to the realisation of gains at rates before the increases under the 1986 Act came into effect.

Some opponents of a cut in capital gains tax admit that a rate reduction boosts short-term tax yields but then argue that the observed increase merely reflects a change in the timing of realisations that would ultimately occur at higher tax rates. Today's tax gains from a cut, they contend, simply would be at the expense of higher tax payments in the future under current rates.

The primary focus of the debate over the capital gains tax is the predicted effect on tax revenues. As the debate has become more intense, the economic research on the subject has become more extensive and systematic, but unfortunately also more complex and arcane. Neverthe-

Table 3

Capital Gains Realisations and Tax Revenues: USA, 1954–1989

Year	Capital Gains Realisations $ billions	Tax revenue $ billions	Marginal tax rate %
1954	7.157	1.010	25.00
1955	9.881	1.465	25.00
1956	9.683	1.402	25.00
1957	8.110	1.115	25.00
1958	9.440	1.309	25.00
1959	13.137	1.920	25.00
1960	11.747	1.687	25.00
1961	16.001	2.481	25.00
1962	13.451	1.954	25.00
1963	14.579	2.143	25.00
1964	17.431	2.482	25.00
1965	21.484	3.003	25.00
1966	21.348	2.905	25.00
1967	27.535	4.112	25.00
1968	35.607	5.943	25.00
1969	31.439	5.275	25.00
1970	20.848	3.161	25.00
1971	28.341	4.350	25.00
1972	35.869	5.708	25.00
1973	35.757	5.366	25.00
1974	30.217	4.253	25.00
1975	30.903	4.534	25.00
1976	39.492	6.621	33.49
1977	45.337	8.104	33.77
1978	50.526	9.104	34.13
1979	73.443	11.669	25.97
1980	74.582	12.459	26.67
1981	80.938	12.684	24.81
1982	90.153	12.900	20.00
1983	119.118	18.468	20.00
1984	138.658	21.534	20.00
1985	168.570	24.495	20.00
1986	326.300	49.700	20.00
1987	144.200	32.900	28.00
1988	161.900	38.900	28.00
1989*	151.800	37.600	28.00

* Preliminary

Source: US Treasury.

less, a review of the most recent studies suggests that the weight of evidence is shifting in favour of those analysts who argue that revenues will not decline if rates are cut.

The Revenue Impact Debate

A 1987 review of the academic literature by Harvard economist Lawrence B. Lindsey concludes that it is extremely unlikely that the capital gains tax increase in the Tax Reform Act of 1986 will produce any additional tax revenue.[10] Most likely, he says, it will produce less revenue than the much lower tax rates of the old law.

According to Lindsey, all but one of the academic studies he reviewed predict 1987-91 revenue losses in the range of $27 to $105 billion when compared with what would have occurred under previous law. Lindsey notes that these same academic studies imply that the capital gains tax rate that would yield the most revenue lies in the range of 9 to 21 per cent. This finding has led most of the sponsors of a rate cut to settle on a 15 per cent rate.

A 1988 study by the Congressional Budget Office (CBO) disputes this reasoning.[11] Although the study found that changes in rates of tax on capital gains produce a significant change in the behaviour of investors, it would not be sufficient to generate higher revenues from lowering the rate of tax on capital gains to 15 per cent. But the authors of the study note the crucial caveat that their statistical estimates are sufficiently imprecise that a conclusion that lower rates will raise revenues cannot be ruled out.

The revenue impact debate currently centres on an updated study recently completed by the US Treasury.[12] The original Treasury study, completed in 1985, concluded that:

'The available statistical evidence shows that the reduction in tax rates on capital gains in the 1978 Act caused a substantial increase in revenue from capital gains taxes in the first year after the tax cut, and in the long

---

[10] Lawrence B. Lindsey, *Capital Gains Taxes Under the Tax Reform Act of 1986: Revenue Estimates Under Various Assumptions,* Cambridge, Mass.: National Bureau of Economic Research, Working Paper No. 2215, 1987.

[11] *How Capital Gains Rates Affect Revenues: The Historical Evidence,* Washington DC: The Congressional Budget Office, March 1988.

[12] Michael R. Darby, Robert Gillingham and John S. Greenlees, *The Direct Revenue Effects of Capital Gains Taxation: A Reconsideration of the Time Series Evidence,* Washington DC: US Treasury, Research Paper No. 8801, May 1988.

run either increased or only slightly decreased the annual Federal revenue from capital gains taxes.'[13]

The 1988 study came essentially to the same conclusion regarding the 1981 capital gains tax rate cuts, but the reluctance of tax critics to accept the broad conclusions of the 1985 study led the Treasury to update its findings. The 1988 report concludes:

'When we extend the original Treasury specifications through 1985, the results imply that the 1978 act produced large and continuing direct revenue gains. Extension of the sample and correction of the flaw in the Treasury report's measurement of inflationary GNP dramatically reduce the estimated losses from the 1981 changes. Finally, substitution of clearly superior regression specifications taken from the 1988 CBO study yields the conclusion that both acts were significantly revenue enhancing.'[14]

These results were immediately challenged by the opponents, and that challenge was met just as quickly by the authors.[15] As Joseph Minarik, a critic of the Treasury studies, observes in his most recent critique, 'The battle over capital gains taxation will probably last as long as we own our income tax'.[16] And so the battle continues, but with the weight of evidence growing in favour of the proposition that a capital gains tax rate cut will not result in a loss of revenue and may even result in a gain.

6. Tax Revenues and Fairness: Who Wins?

Closely related to the issue of revenue is that of fairness: Who would receive the benefit of a rate reduction and how would this change their tax obligations? Few myths are as enduring as the belief that reductions in the capital gains tax rate shift the tax burden from the rich to the poor. Opponents of capital gains tax rate cuts assert that the rich would receive a disproportionate share of the capital gains realisations and most of the benefits. By their definitions, the critics note that the wealthiest 2 per

[13] *Report to Congress on the Capital Gains Tax Rate Reductions of 1978,* US Treasury Dept., September 1985.

[14] Darby *et al., op. cit.,* pp.2-3.

[15] Joseph Minarik, 'The New Treasury Capital Gains Study: What is in the Black Box?', *Tax Notes,* 20 June 1988; and Michael R. Darby, Robert Gillingham and John S. Greenlees, 'The Black Box Revealed: Reply to Minarik', *Tax Notes,* 25 July 1988.

[16] Minarik, *op. cit.,* p.1,471.

cent of the population receive more than a quarter of their annual income in the form of capital gains and that nearly 75 per cent of all capital gains realisations are received by taxpayers with incomes over $100,000, while 45 per cent of such gains go to those with incomes in excess of $500,000. One such critic notes that President Bush's proposal would 'save' the richest taxpayers at least $25,000 a year but save only $20 for most of those earning $60,000 or less.[17]

Supporters of the rate cut respond that such tax rate reductions would actually increase tax payments from the wealthy because it would induce them to shift their wealth from tax shelters to taxable investments and to 'unlock' gains that were not realised because of high taxes. The evidence supports this assessment. Past cuts in tax rates have led to substantial increases in capital gains realisations and tax payments, and an increased share of these tax payments comes from upper-bracket taxpayers. Table 4 demonstrates this conclusion.

Table 4

Percentage Increases in Capital Gains Tax Payments by Adjusted Gross Income: USA, 1980–1984

Adjusted gross income	Taxes paid on capital gains $ thousands		Percentage increase 1980–1984
	1980	1984	
$0–20,000	422,097	574,917	36
20,000 – 75,000	1,847,440	2,543,912	37
75,000 – 200,000	1,915,221	3,478,397	82
200,000 – 500,000	1,443,513	3,405,787	136
500,000+	2,363,446	9,598,114	306

Source: Estimated by the Office of Tax Policy, US Chamber of Commerce, using Statistics of Income, Internal Revenue Service.

As the Table indicates, the tax payments by the richest segment increased by more than eight times as much as those of the lowest income group. Critics may contend that the rise in revenues merely reflects the improving stock market over the period and that the largest

[17] *Robert S. McIntyre, Statement before the Senate Finance Committee, 14 March 1989.*

single source of capital gains realisations is sales of common stock. But such a contention is not supported by the facts. Over the period covered in the Table, the New York Stock Exchange Composite Index rose by just 36 per cent compared with the 306 per cent increase in tax payments by the richest income group. Revenue increases of this magnitude reflect increased unlocking of gains, proportionately more investment in taxable assets and greater mobility of capital.

Table 4 also demonstrates that the cut in taxes actually shifted the tax burden towards the richest groups, in contrast to the popular wisdom. Between 1980 and 1984, the share of capital gains taxes paid by taxpayers earning $20,000 or less declined from 5.3 to 2.9 per cent, while the share of taxpayers reporting incomes of $500,000 or more rose from 29.6 to 48.6 per cent of all taxes paid on capital gains.

While Table 4 and its analysis demonstrate the extent to which capital gains tax rate reductions lead to proportionately greater tax payments by the higher-income households, such aggregate data as are presented in Table 4 overstate the extent to which capital gains realisations are experienced by the wealthier households. In fact, capital gains realisations tend to be spread rather evenly throughout the income distribution when the income distribution is defined to include only 'recurring' income - that is, reported income less capital gains realisations.

This distinction in the measurement of income is important. For many individuals, capital gains realisations are infrequent occurrences and reflect a unique one-off event that makes the taxpayer appear rich for one year by pushing him into higher income brackets. Realised capital gains tend often to be such non-recurring events as: the sale of a small business upon retirement; an elderly widow liquidating her husband's accumulated investments; the sale of stock to buy a house or pay for a child's college tuition; or the liquidation of an investment portfolio in anticipation of an economic downturn. When aggregated with other income, these give the appearance of being received almost exclusively by the very rich.

Table 5 shows the relationship of capital gains realisations to levels of income net of capital gains. With this correction, it can be seen that realised capital gains are distributed rather evenly throughout the income distribution. More than a quarter of realisations were experienced by households earning $20,000 or less, and households earning less than $75,000 received more than half of realised capital gains. Thus, in stark contrast to the claims of the critics, a capital gains tax rate reduction would provide significant benefits to all income levels, not just to the affluent.

Table 5

Distribution of Capital Gains by Recurring Income: USA, 1985

Income group $ thousands	Capital gains $ millions	Per cent of all gains
Under 10	35.30	20.79
10 – 20	8.90	5.24
20 – 30	10.70	6.30
30 – 40	10.10	5.95
40 – 50	11.10	6.54
50 – 75	17.50	10.31
75 – 100	12.50	7.36
100 – 150	13.10	7.71
150 – 200	8.70	5.12
Over 200	41.90	24.68
Total	169.80	100.00

Source: US Internal Revenue Service, 1985 Individual Tax Model File, Public Use Sample.

7. The Proposals Before Congress

As was explained under Section 2 above (p.45), the probability of a major reduction in rates of capital gains tax has been falling over the last two years or so. The theme of this Chapter is that this change in the political climate is in conflict with economic logic and with the empirical evidence. The pressure for reform is bound to increase again. So what are the proposals for reform put forward in recent years, and what are their relative merits?

Nearly a dozen proposals to reduce the rate have been introduced in this Congress. The proposals differ widely in coverage, holding period, rate reduction, complexity and economic impact. To evaluate rival measures, lawmakers need to judge them against a set of base criteria. Amongst the most important of these are tax rates, holding period and coverage.

Tax Rates

Since a key goal of a tax cut must be to stimulate the greatest volume of investment with the minimum revenue loss to the Treasury, preference should be given to those proposals that cut the tax rate as deeply as possible while still leaving it within Professor Lindsey's estimated revenue-maximising range of 9 to 21 per cent. With 15 per cent as the mid-point of this range, proposals which include rate cuts to 15 per cent or less should be preferred. President Bush's proposal, with rates ranging between 0 and 15 per cent, and H.R.461 and H.R.499, with flat rates of 15 per cent, lead the list. S.171 with its implied top rate of 16.5 per cent is close to this group of leading measures.

Holding Period

In principle there should be no required holding period before an asset becomes eligible for taxation as a capital gain instead of as ordinary income. Required holding periods serve no useful economic purpose and probably distort investment patterns in a counterproductive direction. In practice, however, the tax code has made a distinction between short-term and long-term capital gains, with the preferential rates being applied to the latter as a disincentive to speculation. Qualifying periods have varied from a low of three months to as long as one year. Currently the qualifying period is six months.

A popular, though unverified, notion holds that many of America's competitive problems stem from the 'shortsightedness' of its business managers. The lengthy holding periods in several of the proposals represent a peculiar, though ineffective, way of curing this alleged failing. In fact, few other industrialised countries, including the 'far-sighted' Japanese, make such a distinction.

The many capital gains proposals under consideration contain required holding periods ranging from none in H.R.461 and one year for H.R.499 and S.171 to four years for S.348. Inasmuch as all these proposals seek to encourage entrepreneurial start-ups, the lengthy holding period could discourage such investments. Even a one-year required holding period might be too long. With the average post-war business cycle averaging five years, the four- and five-year holding periods required by several of the proposals could shift needed investment away from new firms in favour of mature companies.

Coverage

In an effort to target the tax incentive on preferred forms of economic activity, each of the legislative proposals would limit the preference to certain types of investments. For instance, S.171 covers only common stock, S.348 covers newly issued common stock in firms with less than $100 million paid in capital, while the Bush plan covers all common stocks as well as bonds, land and non-depreciable real property. S.551, H.R.461 and H.R.499 are the most inclusive in coverage, with the latter two proposals including virtually all assets. Excluded from many plans are 'collectables' and depreciable real estate such as office building and apartment complexes. Owner-occupied housing is also excluded; but existing preferences in the tax code serve effectively to shelter realised capital gains on houses.

As with the holding period, the exclusion of certain types of assets distorts investment decisions and leads to an inefficient allocation of capital resources. Bonds are held by investors for their potential capital gain as well as interest income. Precluding them from capital gains taxation could raise bond interest rates relatively to the return on equities and penalise those firms dependent upon debt for capital. This interest rate burden would fall more heavily upon the mature and troubled industries with limited access to equity markets. It also could lead to immediate wealth losses for individuals and institutions (such as pension funds) with bonds in their portfolios.

S.348 would extend the capital gains tax preference only to the newly issued shares of businesses with paid-in capital of less than $100 million, in order to target assistance on new and growing small businesses. But although new ventures play a vital role in a dynamic economy, there is no particularly good economic reason to assist them at the expense of their larger competitors. Such discrimination could lead to serious distortions, misallocating capital throughout the economy and encouraging costly and unproductive corporate restructurings to take advantage of the tax rate reduction on special classes of shares.

Proposals such as S.348 would also create complexities among new and existing shareholders of eligible companies and these complexities and uncertainties could offset in whole or in part the benefits of the more favourable capital gains tax treatment. Growing companies generally issue their shares in increments over their first several years of existence as the need for capital arises and as they become better established in the market. Because newly issued shares would under S.348 be sold with the one-time capital gains tax preference, existing shares - which now would sell without the preference - would decline in value in secondary trading whenever a new offering was announced. This added uncertainty, combined with the required four-year holding period and relatively high capital gains tax rate, suggests that S.348 would provide very limited incentives to investors and would thus do little to assist new firms in raising capital.

8. Conclusion

The evidence accumulated since the Second World War makes a powerful case in favour of a substantial reduction in the capital gains tax rate. Whether the issue is encouraging savings and investment, fairness or revenue, the data and the studies demonstrate that concerns expressed by critics of a cut are either exaggerated or entirely wrong.

In response to this evidence, the White House and many members of Congress from both political parties have developed proposals and introduced legislation to rectify the mistakes made in the treatment of capital gains by the Tax Reform Act of 1986. While some of these proposals are better than others, collectively they represent a growing appreciation by public officials that low rates make an important contribution to America's economic well-being. This trend should be encouraged and Congress and the White House should work together to craft legislation to apply a lower tax rate to gains on a broad category of financial and tangible assets. The setbacks in implementing reforms over the last two years illustrate the main thesis of 'Public choice' theory, that particular interests may prevail over the interests of the economy and the population in general. This Chapter has explained why particular interests have prevailed in the short term and why this situation should be reversed.

OTHER SOURCES FOR CAPITAL GAINS TAX REFORM IN THE UNITED STATES

Andersson, Krister, 'Implications of a lower capital gains tax rate in the United States', IMF WP/89/100.

Bolster, Paul J., Lawrence B. Lindsey, Andrew W. Mitrusi, *Tax induced trading: the effect of the 1986 Tax Reform Act on stock market activity*, National Bureau of Economic Research, Inc., Working Paper No. 2659, 1988.

Boskin, Michael J. (Chairman, Council of Economic Advisers), Testimony before the Senate Finance Committee, 28 March 1990.

Gideon, Kenneth W. (Assistant Secretary, Tax Policy), Statement before the Committee on Finance, United States Senate, 28 March 1990.

Gravelle, Jane G., and Lawrence B. Lindsey, 'Capital gains: special report', Tax Notes, 25 January 1988.

Heritage Foundation, The, 'Taxation of Capital Gains', Hearing before members of the Committee on Ways and Means, US House of Representatives, 2 February 1988.

Lindsey, Lawrence B., 'Capital Gains Rates, Realizations and Revenues', Chapter 3 of Martin Feldstein (ed.), *The Effects of Taxation on Capital Accumulation*, Chicago: University of Chicago Press, 1987 (NBER WP 1017).

5

CAPITAL GAINS TAX: REFORM THROUGH ABOLITION

Barry Bracewell-Milnes

1. Introduction

IN HIS 1988 BUDGET, Chancellor of the Exchequer Nigel Lawson aligned the rates of capital gains tax with those of income tax (above their respective thresholds) and thus raised the rate of capital gains tax for the majority of taxpayers from 30 per cent to 40 per cent. In his 1989 Budget, he abolished hold-over relief for capital gains tax on lifetime gifts, thereby re-introducing for the majority of taxpayers (and at a higher rate) the tax on lifetime gifts which he had abolished only three years earlier. All this was sharply at variance with the thrust of the present Government's tax policy. With the exception of capital gains tax, no rate of tax on income or capital has been increased since 1979 and no new tax on income or capital has been introduced, except to combat what the Government regarded as tax avoidance.

Supporters of the alignment of capital gains tax rates with those of income tax are of three main kinds. There are socialists and collectivists, who tend to favour any increase in taxes on capital in private hands; there are the Inland Revenue, who are now spared most of their previous work in deciding whether a transaction constitutes income or a capital gain; and there are the *horophobes* or boundary-haters. Now, any tax jurisdiction that levies a tax on income has a problem with the boundary between income and capital gains, and this problem has to be resolved somehow; but it does not follow that the best solution is to obliterate the boundary by aligning capital gains tax with income tax or *vice versa.*

This is the worst solution rather than the best. It is the fiscal equivalent of the 20th-century practice of total war by contrast with the 18th-century practice of limited conflicts. It is as though boundary disputes concerning Alsace and Lorraine could be resolved, not by limited boundary adjustments, but only by the absorption either of Germany into France or of France into Germany.

Chancellor Lawson's 'Horophobia'

Chancellor Lawson was by his own admission a *horophobe*. In *Tax Reform: the Government's Record*[1] he stated:

> 'In this year's Budget I have ... made the marginal rates of capital gains tax the same as the marginal rates of income tax ... . These changes can only help to promote more sensible savings and investment decisions.'

It is the thesis of the present paper that these changes will serve to achieve the opposite. Chancellor Lawson's *horophobia* has led him into a blind alley, because he has not recognised sufficiently, if at all, the enormous costs imposed by the abolition of the boundary between marginal rates of tax on income and capital gains – not only financial costs but costs in terms of social cohesion and justice between taxpayers. The only way forward for the Treasury is to leave this impasse by the route it was entered.

A number of tax policy questions which have been the subject of lively debate over the last generation are now effectively settled for the foreseeable future. There is little or no pressure for the re-introduction of the 1965-style 'classical' system of corporation tax, for example, with its systematic double taxation of company and shareholder, nor for the restoration of the more generous capital allowances available before 1984. By contrast, it is realistic to hope that the increases and extensions of capital gains tax in 1988 and 1989 will not long survive the tenure of office of the Chancellor who introduced them.[2] The damage done by the present system is too great to admit of its passive acceptance by business or free-market lobbyists; and its defence among supporters of the free market consists of no more than the flimsy edifice of the boundary argument.

---

[1] Conservative Political Centre Bookshop, London, July 1988.

[2] A robust critique of the present capital gains tax was contained in Thomas Griffin's *What's Wrong with Capital Gains Tax?*, London: Centre for Policy Studies, 1991.

The present paper discusses the cost of yielding to this argument; argues the case for abolition as the only radical solution to the problem of capital gains tax; and puts forward a number of short-term proposals which would be compatible with the present structure of the tax while at the same time constituting steps towards its eventual abolition.

2. British Political and Fiscal Background

In an historical perspective, the taxation of capital gains is alien to the British fiscal tradition. The introduction of a capital gains tax first attracted widespread public interest as a result of the work of the Royal Commission on the Taxation of Profits and Income.[3] The Royal Commission divided on party-political lines, the Majority favouring a sharp distinction between income and capital gains, while the Minority recommended the introduction of a capital gains tax. This idea was taken up by the Minority's colleagues in the Labour Party, and a capital gains tax was introduced in 1965, within a year of Labour's return to power.

The Minority's case was based on the boundary argument – that is, the anomalies involved in drawing a sharp distinction between income and capital gains in any particular place. However, they inconsistently proposed a boundary of their own.

'We think therefore that the taxation of capital gains beyond a certain rate would have highly undesirable effects on risk-bearing, saving and capital formation. ...We therefore recommend that ... capital gains should be subjected to income taxation but not to surtax.'[4] (p.374)

The tax which was introduced in 1965, superseding the tax on short-term capital gains of 1962, was yet more favourable to capital gains by comparison with income than the recommendation of the Royal Commission Minority. The standard (basic) rate of income tax was 41.25 per cent (8s 3d); but the rate of capital gains tax was set 11.25 points lower at 30 per cent. The rate of tax on individuals remained at 30 per cent until it was raised to a maximum of 40 per cent in 1988. Since there is no top-slicing for capital gains, gains on assets that are lumpy and not fungible are now generally taxed more heavily than income. Forty per cent is among the highest general rates of tax on capital gains in the world.

---

[3] *Final Report*, Cmd.9474, London: HMSO, June 1955.

[4] In present-day terminology, subjected to the basic rate of income tax but not to the higher rate.

Further Legislative Changes

In the 1965 legislation, death was a deemed disposal constituting an occasion for charge; but this provision ceased to apply for deaths occurring after 31 March 1971. Gilt-edged stocks held for more than a year were exempted (at a time when the market was depressed) in 1969. Roll-over relief for the replacement of business assets was introduced in 1971. Hold-over relief for lifetime gifts between individuals was introduced in 1980 and for gifts into settlement in 1981 and out of settlement in 1982. (These are the reliefs which were abolished in 1989.) In 1982, capital gains tax was indexed by the retail prices index so as to reduce the tax base by the amount of inflationary gains since March 1982; pre-1982 inflationary gains were still taxable. In 1985, British government securities and certain corporate bonds were made exempt assets (from 1986); previously, these assets had been exempt only if held for more than 12 months. In 1986, the basic rate of income tax was reduced to 29 per cent and was for the first time below the rate of capital gains tax. In 1987 the rate of tax on corporate capital gains was raised from 30 to 35 per cent and the tax was rebased from the original 1965 to 1982; pre-1982 gains now fell out of charge instead of pre-1965 gains, which resolved the problem of inflationary gains before 1982. In 1988, individuals' capital gains were made subject to charge at their marginal rates of income tax (without 'top-slicing' or spreading over a period of years) above the exempt annual amount of capital gains, which was reduced from £6,600 to £5,000. In 1989, hold-over relief for lifetime gifts was abolished except for certain gifts of business, agricultural and heritage assets. In 1991 limited provision was made for setting trade losses against the capital gains of unincorporated traders. Existing law has been consolidated in the Taxation of Chargeable Gains Act 1992.

These many changes, and others, reflect the wide divergences of opinion about the tax and the financial and political pressure points to which it gives rise. It is notable that Nigel Lawson's 1988 reform of capital gains tax, with its increase in the rate of tax levied on a base narrowed by indexation, was founded on the opposite principle from that of his 1984 reform of corporation tax (lower tax rates on a base broadened by the reduction of capital allowances). The reform of capital gains tax in 1988 ignored the supply-side argument entirely.

This lack of consensus about whether and how to tax capital gains is also reflected in a wide variety of treatment within the countries of the OECD. Corporate gains are often taxed more heavily than the gains of individuals; and real property is often taxed more heavily than movable assets. Sandford, in his study of 22 OECD countries,[5] identifies four countries with a separate capital gains tax (Denmark, Ireland, Portugal, United Kingdom), in addition to Switzerland, where all 26 cantons tax gains on private immovable property and eight cantons tax gains on private movables. The other 17 countries tax capital gains, if at all, as part of the income tax régime. There are no special provisions in three countries; and in a further four, capital gains taxation is mainly restricted to short-term or speculative gains. In the remaining 10 countries, a wide range of capital gains is subject to income tax. However, a principal difference between the UK and other countries is that all the other European countries that levy tax on capital gains have some form of taper or time limit; the UK is the only country that provides no exemption or lower tax rate in recognition of the length of the holding period. Capital gains tax constitutes a competitive disadvantage for the UK by comparison with almost all the other countries of the OECD.

3. The Statistical Background

The yield of capital gains tax on individuals and trustees was forecast at £1.1 billion for 1992-93, which compares with up to £2.2 billion for the full-year cost of a 1p reduction in the basic rate of income tax and a £28 billion forecast for the public sector borrowing requirement in 1992-93. Thus capital gains tax is not important as a revenue raiser.

About two-thirds of the yield in 1990-91 arose from gains on shares and other financial assets, with the remainder attributable to gains on land, property and other tangible assets.[6] Thus the main impact of the tax is on shares and other financial assets.

The proportion of capital gains tax receipts attributable to the higher rate of 40 per cent was about half in 1989-90 and had risen to three-quarters in 1990-91 as the change of system in 1988 continued to take effect.[7] The proportion may be higher than three-quarters in 1991-92. Thus under the present system capital gains are taxed predominantly at 40 per cent.

Capital gains tax was assessed on 137,000 individuals and 17,000 trusts for disposals in 1987-88 (the latest full year for which the figures

---

[5] C.T. Sandford, *Taxation of Net Wealth, Capital Transfers and Capital Gains of Individuals*, Paris: Organisation for Economic Co-operation and Development, 1988. See Chapter 3, above, pp.31-43, especially Table 1, p.33.

[6] *House of Commons Hansard*, Written Answers, 7 May 1991, cols.381-382.

[7] *Ibid.*

are available), less than a tenth of the 1.5 million or so currently paying the higher rate of income tax, and less than a hundredth of the 22.4 million income tax payers in 1987-88. Thus capital gains tax payers are not important numerically, which may be their weakness politically. Of these 154,000 taxpayers, 17,300 or 11 per cent were assessed on chargeable gains of £7,123 million or 70 per cent of the total and 1,400 or less than 1 per cent contributed £1,000 million or 36 per cent of the yield. But the inference that capital gains tax is paid predominantly by the rich or very rich would be incorrect. Many of these taxpayers may be assumed to attract a heavy tax liability by virtue, not of large regular income, but of large exceptional capital gains. Lindsey cites a detailed analysis of 1984 gains in the United States showing that 43 per cent of taxpayers with gains over $100,000 had ordinary, recurring income of $50,000 or less. Capital gains tax is also disproportionately a tax on the old. Under the US Tax Reform Act of 1986, taxpayers over 65 pay about 11 per cent of the total income tax but more than 26 per cent of the capital gains tax.[8] In the UK in 1988-89, income tax paid by the elderly was 9 per cent of income tax; capital gains tax paid by taxpayers over 65 was 22 per cent of the total (excluding taxpayers of unknown age), thus more than twice as much (the same relationship as in the United States).

Supply-side material is discussed in Chapter 4. As has been pointed out by Griffin,[9] some consensus has recently been achieved in support of a reduction in rates: of 14 studies listed by the Department of the Treasury's Office of Tax Analysis, most of those published in the last three years predict a modest to a very positive long-run revenue gain.

4. The Academic Background

Like many other economic terms, 'income' has a number of different meanings, suitable for a number of different purposes. Accounting income may differ from taxable income; accrued income may differ from income received; annual income may differ from income net of losses carried forward; domestic income on the territorial basis may differ from world-wide income; income adjusted for inflation may differ from income not so adjusted; and so on.

The definition of income, for purposes of tax policy or anything else, is best approached in full recognition of these differences. The task on hand, whatever it may be, should influence or shape the definition of

---

[8] Lawrence B. Lindsey, *The Growth Experiment*, New York: Basic Books, 1990, pp.188-89.

[9] *What's Wrong with Capital Gains Tax?*, *op. cit.*

income to be used; an inappropriate definition of income will prejudge and colour policy decisions that ought to be taken on their merits. Like alcohol, the concept of income is a good servant and a bad master.

A contrary view goes back in the academic tradition at least to Henry Simons, whose *Personal Income Taxation*[10] states that

'Personal income may be defined as the algebraic sum of (1) the market value of rights exercised in consumption and (2) the change in the value of the store of property rights between the beginning and end of the period in question' (p.50).

This may be translated into plain words as the arithmetic (why algebraic?) sum of consumption, new saving and capital gains. If anyone is interested in the rather recondite magnitude of the sum of consumption and additions to wealth, Simons's long-winded formulation defines it by tautology. But the question remains just what, if anything, all this has to do with income.

The thrust of Simons's book is a diatribe against everyone who wishes to tax capital gains less heavily than income. No deviation from his 'algebraic' sum is tolerated. But his position is flawed at both the theoretical and practical levels. *At the theoretical level*, for example, he does not believe his own doctrine that there is a single, comprehensive definition of income as a taxable base. He is an enthusiast for taxes on capital transfers: 'There is now little dispute as to the propriety of taxing gifts, inheritances and bequests' (p.126). However,

'whether lottery prizes or "unearned increments" are taxed as such is largely irrelevant to the question of whether they should be brought into the calculation of taxable personal income. And the same must be said of gifts, inheritances and bequests' (p.128).

Hear, hear! And the same must be said of capital gains. *At the practical level*, for example, Simons made no allowance for inflation, which was an understandable omission in 1938. But, in the many tax jurisdictions where inflation is a problem, should a comprehensive Simons-style (or 'Haig-Simons') income tax base make allowance for inflation in the tax base of capital gains but not of income (as in the UK) or of neither (as in the United States) or of income only or of both? There are few, if any, tax jurisdictions in the world that have obliterated the distinction between capital gains and income in the manner Simons recommended;

---

[10] Chicago: University of Chicago Press, 1938.

and the practical reasons for this outcome have a sound theoretical basis.

Simons did good work in other areas of economics; and it is a pity that this has been overshadowed by his contribution to fiscal theory: *the evil that men do lives after them; the good is oft intérred with their bones.* Fortunately, the opposite academic tradition, that income and capital gains are different in nature though making contact at the boundary, is not only deeply rooted (Fisher, Bittker and others) but also flourishing as never before (Lindsey: see under '5. The capital gains tax quandary', below, and in Chapter 4, above, pp.56-57).

5. The Capital Gains Tax Quandary

At the boundary with income, capital gains may have the nature of income and be taxed as such. Examples are gains from activities of a trading nature and gains predetermined in amount and period of maturity; both were already taxed as income in the UK before the capital gains tax changes of 1988. But this no-man's land between income and capital gains is a narrow zone, wherever the boundary may be drawn. Most income is payable regularly, at least once a year and often more frequently. Most non-trading income is predictable in amount without much inaccuracy. Most non-trading capital gains accrue over substantial periods and are unpredictable in amount and even direction (they may turn out to be losses). Nor does it help to redefine all capital gains as trading income; it is contrary to common-sense to characterise as trading income a profit on the sale of a house, for example, after 30 years of owner-occupation.

Outside a narrow boundary zone, income and capital gains are different in nature. The confusion of capital gains with income is an exploitation of the old Greek sophists' trick known as *sorites*. How many pebbles make a heap? One pebble, two pebbles, three pebbles...? Alternatively, if we start with a heap of 100 pebbles and keep taking one away, when does the heap cease to be a heap? How many hairs can a man have on his head and still be bald? One hair, two hairs, three hairs...ten thousand hairs? Common sense has no difficulty in making these distinctions. Some men are bald, others are not; similarly, night can be distinguished from day, even though the one changes gradually into the other.

The fundamental differences between income and capital gains account for the structure of capital gains taxes in practice and explain why, outside a narrow boundary zone with income, capital gains are not a satisfactory tax base at all. The first problem is that of *accruals*. For many types of income, the distinction between accruals and realisations is of minor importance because income is received regularly and frequently; where the distinction is important, there are practical ways of dealing with it (such as 'equalisation' for dividends and the distinction between the receipts basis and the accruals basis of taxing trading income). For capital gains, it is quite another story. For example, many owner-occupiers and other passive investors accrue gains for a generation or more before they are realised; and, unlike all forms of non-trading income, accrued gains can be substantially negative (that is, losses), as after a stock exchange crash or a slump in property prices.[11]

For most capital gains, accruals would be an intolerable tax base both for the taxpayer and for the government. For the taxpayer, the compliance costs would be enormous, since many taxpayers neither require nor obtain annual or other frequent valuations of their assets; there would also be a major fiscal distortion, since taxpayers would often have to sell assets which they would have preferred to retain in order to pay tax on additional wealth which they did not know they had. The situation would be equally unsatisfactory for the Treasury, since the tax base would vary unpredictably by billions of pounds in either direction as a result of movements in the stock exchange, property prices and prices of other assets. For these and other reasons, accruals have enjoyed little, if any, serious support as the base of a general capital gains tax, even among academics. Simons says: 'Unfortunately, the realization criterion must be accepted as a practical necessity' (p.153). The tone of regret is understandable from Simons's standpoint, since the acceptance of the realisations basis in preference to accruals strikes at the heart of his attempt to tax income comprehensively and equitably.[12]

Capital Gains Realisations Basis

The abandonment of the accruals base takes with it Simons's 'algebraic sum' of consumption and the increase in wealth. Instead we have the sum of income in the common sense and realisations of capital gains. This means a tax on portfolio rearrangements, and this is the cause of the

---

[11] Realisations can also be substantially negative, but less often are so, because owners are reluctant to sell at a loss and retain their assets in the hope that their loss will be reversed.

[12] 'Prevailing methods of measurement do aggravate the inequities. The real culprit here is the realization criterion' (p.153). There are many other such comments, not least in the 'brief consideration of the familiar criterion of realization' (pp.80-90).

'locking-in' effect for which capital gains tax has so often been criticised: if the rearrangement is not to be frustrated by taxation, the prospective value of the new asset for the investor must exceed the prospective value of his existing asset by a margin sufficient to cover the tax; and this will often be impossible, since the condition must be satisfied simultaneously but in reverse for the other parties to the transaction.

Even the realisations basis, if employed symmetrically between taxpayer and fisc, would vary substantially and unpredictably from year to year as a result of changes in asset values and turnover; and it could be negative in a year when asset values fell. But the UK capital gains tax is so structured, or rigged, that the Treasury always makes a profit, year after year, even if taxpayers collectively suffer a loss; so the effective rate of capital gains tax is not the same as that of income tax, but higher. The effective rate of capital gains tax is also higher than that of income tax because of the absence of top-slicing. (See Section 2, above, p.67.) Net capital losses in any year cannot be carried back or offset against liability to income tax or other taxes; they can only be carried forward (without allowance for interest or indexation for inflation) for offset against future gains, and they are extinguished on the death of an individual taxpayer. All the former distinctions between income and capital gains, with their restrictions on the transfer and use of losses, were retained when UK rates of capital gains tax were aligned with those of income tax in 1988. Far from resembling the partnership between fisc and taxpayer which generally characterises the taxation of trading income, capital gains tax is a system of fiscal power without financial responsibility.

The lack of symmetry between fisc and taxpayer extends to the capital dimension and accruals. Capital gains tax is a contingent liability even for taxpayers who may not pay the tax for years; and yet there is no government asset corresponding to this liability, since the government maintains no balance sheet or similar capital account in which such an asset could be included. The taxpayer loses; but the government has no corresponding gain.

The radical differences between income tax and capital gains tax extend to their supply-side effects. Work by the Harvard economist Lawrence Lindsey and others has suggested that the maximum-revenue rate of capital gains tax in the United States is about 15 per cent, as compared with an actual maximum rate of 28 per cent: in other words, the US Treasury would gain tax revenue by reducing the rate of capital gains tax from 28 to 15 per cent.[13] These findings were available but were apparently ignored by the UK Treasury in the preparation of the

1988 Budget. Although Lindsey's findings have been attacked and defended in the United States, Lindsey's own figure for the maximum-revenue rate of income tax is much higher, at about 40 per cent; and few, if any, even of his critics would assert that the maximum-revenue rates for the two taxes are the same.[14]

Finally, the complexity of capital gains tax, which is in a different league from that of income tax, is a further indicator of the difference in nature between the two taxes and the bases on which they are levied. Capital gains tax was already complex when it was introduced in 1965; and, as a result of the various reforms and changes over the last 27 years, it is now not only largely unintelligible to the majority of taxpayers but at least partially so to many professional advisers.

6. The Incidence of Capital Gains Tax

It has long been recognised that the capital gains tax base divides into three parts: inflationary gains, gains from a reduction in the current yield on assets at a constant level of current income, and gains from an increase in current income at a constant level of the current yield. These three parts of the tax base can be combined with each other.

The impact of capital gains tax is on a realised increase in wealth. The incidence, by contrast, corresponds to this threefold classsification.

The incidence of capital gains tax on gains that merely keep pace with the fall in the value of money is a tax on the combination of ownership, realisation and inflation. It is now widely perceived that such a tax base

---

[13] It is worth emphasising that the maximum-revenue rate of tax must be significantly too high for the good of the economy or society as a whole, since at this point the Treasury is not gaining from a marginal increase in the rate of tax whereas the taxpayer is losing from tax-induced changes in economic activity (excess burden). At a significantly lower rate of tax, the marginal increase in government revenue from an increase in the tax rate equals the marginal loss through behavioural changes; in other words, the marginal increase in yield equals the marginal increase in excess burden (or the marginal loss to society excluding transfer payments between taxpayer and Treasury). This rate of tax is a maximum or ceiling under a rational tax policy. (Lawrence Lindsey: *The Growth Experiment*, New York: Basic Books, 1990, Ch.11.) The excess burden of capital gains tax at present levels may be a large multiple of its yield. The US Joint Committee on Taxation estimated that the cuts in tax rates proposed by President Bush would cost $11.4 billion in lost revenue over the next five years but would also reduce excess burden by $100 billion. And according to the Office of Tax Analysis, there would be an increase in tax revenue, not a reduction, so that the Treasury would gain as well as the taxpayer.

[14] Work on this subject by Lindsey and others is cited in Chapter 4. A Parliamentary reply by Francis Maude, MP, Financial Secretary to the Treasury, to David Shaw, MP (*Hansard*, 25 April 1991, col.340) said that studies in the United States were 'not of direct relevance to the United Kingdom, because of differences between the two countries' tax régimes' and added that 'limitations on data would make it difficult to replicate the United States studies in the United Kingdom'.

is both inequitable and economic nonsense. However, the penny took 17 years to drop (1965-82), 17 years during which the annual rate of inflation was always substantial and at its highest almost 30 per cent. During these 17 years, spokesmen of Governments of both main Parties, and many outsiders, argued against the indexation of capital gains tax for inflation on grounds of economics, of equity between taxpayers and of revenue necessity. Nothing is heard of these arguments now; their supporters have been extinct for several years. All this is an encouraging precedent as we turn to the other two elements of the capital gains tax base, which are supported by spokesmen of both main Parties, and many outsiders, on grounds of economics, of equity between taxpayers and of revenue necessity.

The second element of the capital gains tax base is reductions in interest rates or other current yields at constant levels of current income. But interest rates and other yields can rise as well as fall, and this can be true over a long period. Does this in turn mean that the tax yield would be negative over this period? Well, no. The Treasury believe that charity begins at home and have so structured the capital gains tax that, even if the tax base is negative, the tax yield is positive. Indeed, the more the variation about a constant average rate of current yield, the higher the yield of capital gains tax, since the Revenue gain more from reductions in the current yield than they lose from increases. All this shows how civilisation advances. The alchemists merely sought, without success, to turn base metal into gold. The Treasury succeed in extracting gold, not merely from thin air, but from the collective losses of their fellow citizens.

The argument is similar for real gains (capital gains that are not due to inflation or to reductions in interest rates or other current yields on assets). If salaries rise by 10 per cent, for example, and dividends rise by 10 per cent and the value of capital rises by 10 per cent, then the relative position is the same after the change as before if the taxes on salaries and dividends are both proportional and capital gains are free of tax: parity requires that capital gains be untaxed even if earnings and dividends are taxed, since capital gains tax is another layer of tax on savings already subjected to income taxation. Real gains are realised either for re-investment or for consumption. As was noted earlier (above, p.74), gains realised for re-investment are not a suitable base for taxation. A heavier tax on active portfolio management implies a lighter tax on passive portfolio management (or no management at all); such fiscal distortion impairs the efficiency and increases the volatility of the stock market. Moreover, any additional income generated by active portfolio management is subject to income tax in due time; capital gains tax on the present value of this future income is an unthrifty anticipation of tax otherwise payable in due time later on.

Capital gains tax has no valid function in a society and an economy where assets are held for the long term and eventually bequeathed to the next generation. For gains realised for consumption, the argument is different but the conclusion the same. Capital gains used for consumption are postponed consumption, spending out of earlier saving. Tax on these gains can be avoided entirely by not saving the capital that eventually generates the gains but spending it at once. It can also be avoided entirely by not spending the gains but allowing them to accrue. A tax on postponed consumption is a mixed tax on saving and spending which can be entirely avoided, whether by saving less or by saving more. This hybrid tax base can form no part of a logical tax system.

7. Capital Gains Tax and Its Identity Crisis

All other taxes have an identifiable incidence either on spending or on saving or both; for example, inheritance tax and investment income tax on saving, excise duties and value added tax on spending. Even the tax on earned income contains an element of savings tax by comparison with value added tax and other taxes on spending, since it is equivalent to a tax at the same rates on both spending and new saving.

Capital gains tax is the only tax that is sometimes a tax on saving and sometimes a tax on spending. It is a pure tax on saving when it is levied on portfolio re-arrangements. It is a mixed tax on saving and spending when money that could be spent immediately is invested for subsequent spending out of capital growth. It is a pure tax on spending if the gain is eventually realised for consumption.

This crisis of identity derives from the impossibility of taxing accruals; if accruals were taxed each year whether realised or not, capital gains tax would tax saving and spending at the same rates, as the tax on earned income does at present. But since in practice accruals cannot be taxed, capital gains tax is a capricious tax, sometimes taxing saving more heavily than spending and sometimes taxing spending more heavily than saving, and acting mainly to impede the efficient management of the country's capital.

8. Inequity Between Taxpayers

In the literature of public finance, a distinction has been made between horizontal equity (the like treatment of taxpayers in like circumstances) and vertical equity (the unlike treatment of taxpayers in unlike circumstances). The usefulness of these concepts is diminished by the difficulties of construing the terms 'like' and 'unlike'; but the lowest common denominator of agreement is that it is inequitable for a taxpayer with less to be taxed more heavily than a taxpayer with more. Unfortunately, this is just what capital gains tax does, extensively and even systematically, as the following examples show. Capital gains tax is assumed to be levied at 40 per cent, and the original value of the asset is for simplicity assumed to be negligible relatively to the gain.

○ *Accrual versus realisation for spending.* Taxpayer A has accruals of 1,000, tax zero. Taxpayer B realises 100 for spending, tax 40.

○ *Active versus passive portfolio management.* B manages his portfolio actively. He has a gain of 100 on stock X but would prefer to be invested in Y. He pays 40 in tax and invests the remaining 60 in Y. Alternatively, he would be willing to move if he could buy 80 of Y for 100 of X (stock market values being 100 for both), but not if he can buy only 60; so the transaction is fiscally frustrated. A, by contrast, manages his portfolio passively, if at all. His accrued gains of 1,000 are tax-free.[15]

○ *Fungible and non-fungible assets.* Taxpayer A has a portfolio of shares which appreciates by £100,000 over a period of 20 years. A realises his gain at the rate of £5,000 a year and escapes all liability to capital gains tax. Taxpayer B has a property (not of course his principal residence) which appreciates by £50,000 over the same period. Tax at 40 per cent on this gain amounts to £20,000. Tax reduces the smaller gain from 50 per cent of the larger gain to 30 per cent.

○ *The farmer's paradox.* Taxpayer B is a sixth-generation hill farmer in Wales. His income is below the national average; but it is his wish, and that of his family, that the farm should eventually be handed on to the next generation. Land prices double (they were increasing until a few years ago), and soon afterwards he contracts a terminal disease,

---

[15] Section 4 of *What's Wrong with Capital Gains Tax?, op. cit.*, provides a number of examples of how the British tax system gives a strong incentive to hold shares indirectly, through financial institutions exempt from capital gains tax: a larger gain on such assets can attract a smaller tax charge than a smaller gain on assets held directly. It is not surprising that personal share ownership has been declining in Britain throughout the last generation. The institutionalisation of shareholding in Britain is a major cause of the excessive and damaging volatility of the stock market.

from which he dies within a year. Prior to the Finance (No.2) Act 1992, the sole effect on B and his family of the increase in land prices is to increase the charge to inheritance tax at 20 per cent (= 40 per cent minus agricultural property relief at 50 per cent of 40 per cent), so that the increase in land prices which according to Simons makes the family more prosperous in fact obliges them to sell up to 20 per cent of the farm. Taxpayer A is a townsman with twice the national average income from investments through financial houses in agricultural land and other assets. He has no commitment to agricultural land and, when the price doubles, he decides that the time has come to sell. He does so by utilising his annual capital gains tax exemption over a period of several years. At the end of this period neither A nor B has paid any capital gains tax; but A is better off and B's family are worse off as a result of the increase in land prices. So, even though no capital gains tax is paid, the example serves to show why capital gains are an unsuitable base for taxation, since the same gain which confers a benefit on one taxpayer inflicts a loss on another.

○ *The salary earner and the shareholder*. A has a salary of twice the national average income. It is increasing at 5 per cent a year in real terms and is supported by capital investment of 10 times the salary; the capital investment is therefore also increasing at 5 per cent a year, and all the new investment is state-of-the-art. A pays no capital gains or other tax on this new investment. B has an income at the national average from a portfolio of investments. In order to achieve real growth of 5 per cent, he would have to manage his portfolio actively, continually moving into stocks with better prospects, which is the analogue of modernising the investment that supports the salary earner. But, if he did this, he would be paying capital gains tax on a substantial part of his portfolio re-arrangements and would fall further behind A, who already has the larger income; and, if he remained a passive investor in order to avoid capital gains tax, he would fall further behind A for different reasons.

○ *The owner-proprietor: capital gains or dividends*. Proprietors of companies are now encouraged to take money out in the form of dividends, which they can do at an additional tax cost of only 15 per cent, rather than wait for a deferred or more heavily taxed capital gain. There is also a large element of double taxation in capital gains tax on corporate profits, since the tax is levied first on the company and then on the disposal of its shares by its shareholders. As Tom Griffin has pointed out in *What's Wrong with Capital Gains Tax?*, the 1988 charges have in effect moved the balance between income and capital gains to the opposite extreme and encouraged the citizen to spend capital as if it were income. Thus the proprietor who takes a capital gain from his company may pay more tax than if he took a larger sum in dividends.

Similarly, it can be shown that the present régime increases the disadvantage of owning shares directly rather than indirectly through a unit trust, investment trust or other financial intermediary. It increases the already substantial disadvantages of owning wealth in the form of shares by comparison with an owner-occupied house or a pension from employment or self-employment. It increases the fiscal penalty imposed on an entrepreneur by comparison with a passive investor or salary earner. It discourages the enterprise culture and encourages the retirement culture of well-housed, well-pensioned security. And it regularly imposes the heavier tax burden on the poorer taxpayer. For example, A has pension rights with an actuarial value of £250,000, managed tax-free on his behalf. B has invested £50,000 in a property now worth £150,000 which he realises to provide an annuity for his retirement. Capital gains tax reduces this £150,000 to £110,000; as a result of capital gains tax, the value of his retirement annuity falls from 60 per cent of A's to 44 per cent.

All these examples show how capital gains tax can bear more heavily on the poorer taxpayer than on the richer and thus increase the gap between rich and poor; it is not surprising if capital gains tax is more resented than income tax and indeed most other taxes. There are no doubt cases where capital gains tax bears more heavily on the richer taxpayer; but, even if these cases are in a majority, the fact that the distributive results of capital gains tax can so often be perverse is sufficient to disqualify the tax from consideration on grounds of equity.

9. Losses Without Gains

The introduction or abolition of any tax can result in gains and losses, gainers and losers, and normally does so. It is the highest achievement of fiscal policy to put forward a proposal which is *Pareto-optimal*, in the sense that there are gainers but no losers. The distinction of capital gains tax, by contrast, is to be *Pareto-pessimal*, in the sense that there are losers, but few (if any) gainers, or at least that there is a large ratio of losses to gains, of damage done relatively to revenue collected. The reasons why this is so are the theme of this paper; but the main ones are worth highlighting here.

The *American supply-side material* noted in Chapter 4 indicates that the present UK rate of 40 per cent is far above the maximum-revenue rate of the tax; in other words, tax revenue would increase if the UK rate of capital gains tax were reduced. The US data with a top Federal rate of income tax of 28 per cent, an intra-marginal maximum rate of 33 per cent and a maximum-revenue capital gains tax of about 15 per cent suggest that the maximum-revenue rate in the UK might lie within the range 15-20 per cent. But the maximum-revenue rate of a tax is a ceiling rather than a policy target; our other arguments imply a policy target rate of zero.

Because it is impracticable to tax accruals and the only practicable tax base is realisations, capital gains tax is characterised by a massive *locking-in effect*. Taxpayers who would like to dispose of assets are reluctant to precipitate an unnecessary tax charge by so doing. This is *excess burden* or the loss caused by fiscal distortion in addition to the amount of tax collected. Taxpayers lose from the locking-in effect; but the revenue does not gain. Excess burden is likely to be a much larger ratio of the revenue yield for capital gains tax than for most or even all other taxes, because charges to capital gains tax are in general precipitated only by the voluntary and avoidable action of the taxpayer.[16] A large part of capital gains tax liability can be postponed for 30 years or more at a time. Income tax, for example, affects incentives at the margin; capital gains tax can easily frustrate the whole transaction.

Similarly, the *contingent liability to capital gains tax* reduces a taxpayer's real wealth; but the government has no means of enjoying or recording a corresponding increase in its assets (see above, p.74). More generally, capital gains tax, like any tax on capital, reduces the value of assets and a reduction in the rate of tax increases this value.

Capital gains tax has its supporters (collectivists, Inland Revenue administrators and boundary-haters); and these people must obtain some benefit from the tax, even though it is not of a financial character. But a comparison of this benefit with the corresponding costs indicates the high price to the economy and society at which it is purchased.

10. Relationship with Other UK Taxes

Capital gains tax and inheritance tax (or death tax in various forms) are both taxes on capital and are alternatives at least in the sense that Italy and the Netherlands, for example, have inheritance tax but no capital

---

[16] Footnote 13 on p.75 above, cites US research indicating that the excess burden of capital gains tax is some nine times the revenue yield.

gains tax whereas Australia and Canada have capital gains tax but no inheritance tax. Professor Mervyn King and others have recently proposed that the UK inheritance tax should be replaced with a capital gains tax on death (as before 1 April 1971); death would once again become a deemed disposal or occasion for charge to capital gains tax. Since this proposal would replace one death tax with another, and since the yield of capital gains tax on death might well exceed that of inheritance tax, the new tax would in the perspective of the present paper have the disadvantages of inheritance tax as well as its own. From this standpoint, it is regrettable that hold-over relief from capital gains tax was abolished for the majority of lifetime gifts in 1989.

The close relationship between capital gains tax and income tax is a main theme of the present paper. Chancellor Lawson and his successors have already announced and re-affirmed a target income-tax basic rate of 20p. (as compared with the present basic rate of 25p.), and more radical voices are calling for reduction over a period of years to 15p. or 10p. or even for the abolition of the tax. The budgetary arithmetic suggests that this is a serious possibility within a generation or less, if the additional resources becoming available are not absorbed in additional government spending.[17] Since the payment of capital gains tax can be postponed by the taxpayer for a generation or more, this is doubly relevant. First, the locking-in effect is intensified if capital gains tax is linked to a tax in terminal decline. And, second, the harmonisation of the rates of income tax and capital gains tax requires, not their alignment, but their compatibility (as was argued by Chancellor Lawson himself in the context of tax harmonisation within the European Community). By the standards of 1978 (when income tax on investment income rose to 98 per cent and capital gains tax to 30 per cent), income tax at 40 per cent would already be compatible with capital gains tax at zero; and this compatibility would increase as rates of income tax fell. The good prospects for reductions in the rates of income tax therefore strengthen the arguments for abolishing the tax on capital gains.

11. Conclusion and Implications for Policy

This paper has argued that capital gains are different in nature from income, as night differs from day despite the twilight or boundary zones of dawn and dusk. The nature of capital gains makes them an unsuitable base for taxation, outside the boundary zones. Any jurisdiction that

---

[17] This is the theme of *Continuing Tax Reform*, published by the Institute of Directors in 1990.

taxes income has a problem with the boundary between income and capital gains. There is a wide range of possible solutions to this problem, both in theory and in practice: the extension of income taxation to capital gains, in so far as this is possible, is not the best of these solutions, but the worst.

To put the same matter differently, taxation of capital gains at any positive rate, and particularly at full rates of income tax, yields diminishing marginal utility and imposes increasing opportunity costs as the range of capital gains subject to taxation is extended from the pure-income or quasi-income zone of short-term trading gains to embrace longer-term and non-trading gains and eventually (as in the UK at present) all capital gains outside the exempt categories. This paper takes issue with those who deny that there are such increasing opportunity costs and diminishing marginal utility and see nothing wrong in taxing the gain on an asset held for 50 years at the same rate as that on last year's salary. Under the present UK system, the situation is even worse, since there is no top-slicing relief for a long-term capital gain, so that the gain is fully subject to the higher rate of income tax in the year of disposal. And any attempt to align rates of tax on long-term capital gains with those on short-term income violates horizontal and vertical equity within its own terms of reference, because there will almost certainly have been substantial, even major, changes in income tax rates and base over the period of the gain.

Among those who agree that longer-term gains should be taxed less heavily than shorter-term gains (or not at all) and/or that an extension of the concept of 'trading' should not be used as a surrogate for the taxation of long-term non-trading gains and/or that portfolio re-arrangements should be exempt from capital gains tax, there are elements of common purpose. The common purpose is to recognise the distinction between the taxation of income and capital gains to the advantage of the latter. Just where and how the distinction should be drawn is a partly technical but largely political question on which opinions will inevitably differ (although the case for taxing gains is weakest where they are unpredictable and may in the event prove to be losses). It is not the purpose of the present paper to settle such disputes, except that the logic of its argument is to limit to the minimum the base and rates of both income tax and capital gains tax. A few policy proposals in this sense are listed under (A) below; they are not intended to be comprehensive.

There is no such common purpose between those who would wish to abolish capital gains tax and those who would wish to align it with income tax. Nevertheless, if it is possible over the Budgets of the next

10 or 20 years to reduce the base or rates of income tax so as to prevent the tax burden from rising and even to bring it down in accordance with present Government policy, a diplomatic alliance becomes possible between these opposite parties. A few policy proposals in this sense are listed under (B) below; they are not intended to be comprehensive.

(A) Reductions in Capital Gains Tax Compatible with its Abolition

1. Exemption of portfolio re-arrangements, defined as the replacement of one chargeable asset with another; this would remove a major disadvantage of individual relatively to institutional investors.

2. Exemption of assets held for more than a stated period, preferably with a taper of the rate of charge within the period.

3. Regular rebasing of the tax (which was rebased from 1965 to 1982 in 1987). Regular rebasing could for some purposes be an alternative to exemption of assets held for more than a stated period.

4. Specification of the rates of capital gains tax independently of the rates of income tax. This reform would still be desirable even if, for the time being, the separately specified rates of income tax and capital gains tax remained the same.

5. Reduction in the present rates of capital gains tax to a single rate below the basic rate of income tax.

6. Re-introduction of hold-over relief on disposals by way of lifetime gifts.

(B) Reductions in Capital Gains Tax Compatible with its Continued Existence

7. Unlimited carry-back of losses; present restrictions on the use of losses raise the effective rate of the tax and illustrate the Revenue's preference for sharing the taxpayer's gains while avoiding a share in his losses.

8. Increase and indexation of annual exempt amount.

9. Provision for unused annual exemption to be carried forward.

10. Increases in the amounts of retirement relief from capital gains tax and removal of the present age limits for retirement relief.

11. Exemption of all shares in unquoted companies and other business

assets or exemption of business assets (including interests of 25 per cent or less) in the hands of their managers or extension of Personal Equity Plans (PEPs) to cover shares in unquoted companies or at least shares owned by the managers of the company.

12. A 1 per cent turnover tax as an alternative to capital gains tax, at the taxpayer's option, following the precedent set by Japan.

12. Summary

The difficulty of the boundary between income and capital gains is not a good reason for assimilating the taxation of capital gains to that of income or indeed (outside a narrow boundary zone) for taxing capital gains at all. Capital gains are radically different from income, and attempts to apply the same tax regime to both are flawed at the theoretical and practical levels. These flaws are illustrated by a wide range of inequitable results (in which the taxation of capital gains imposes a heavier burden on the poorer taxpayer and a lighter burden on the richer). Capital gains tax also imposes an exceptionally heavy excess burden, or ratio of losses to gains, not least through the damage it does to enterprise and the enterprise culture. United States research suggests that the present UK 40 per cent rate of capital gains tax may be more than twice the maximum-revenue rate, so that the yield of the tax would be increased if the rate were cut to 20 per cent or below. The paper ends with a number of reforms that would mitigate the harshness of the present tax or serve as steps towards its abolition.

THE AUTHORS

Adrian Beecroft joined ICL on leaving Oxford with a first-class honours degree in Physics. After programming and systems design experience, he became an account executive. Prior to leaving in 1973, he was responsible for the sales and support team working with ICL's largest commercial customer.

He then joined Ocean Transport & Trading Ltd, where he was responsible for new ventures and acquisitions. Adrian was awarded a Harkness Fellowship to Harvard Business School in 1974. On graduating as a Baker Scholar in 1976, he joined the Boston Consulting Group (BCG) where he worked until he joined Apax Partners in 1984. He became a Vice-President of BCG in 1982 and was responsible for leading strategy reviews for major British, European, American and Japanese companies. He specialised in high technology businesses, and in companies in the retail and distribution area, and he has continued to work in these areas with Apax.

As a director of Apax, Adrian is responsible for identifying and negotiating investment opportunities. He has represented Apax on the boards of a number of public and private companies. He was appointed Chairman of the British Venture Capital Association in 1991.

Barry Bracewell-Milnes was educated at Uppingham School, at New College, Oxford, where he read Classical Moderations and then changed to Economics, and at King's College, Cambridge, where he took his doctorate.

Dr Bracewell-Milnes now works as a consultant to academic and industrial bodies on government and international fiscal and economic policy. He was Economic Director of the Confederation of British Industry, 1968-73. Since leaving the CBI he has been Economic Adviser to The Institute of Directors, and his other appointments during the period have included Economic Consultant to the Fiscal-Economic Institute, Erasmus University, Rotterdam.

He is the author of over a dozen books on taxation and other economic subjects, including *The Measurement of Fiscal Policy: An Analysis of Tax Systems in Terms of the Political Distinction between 'Right' and 'Left'* (1971); *Is Capital Taxation Fair? The Tradition and the Truth*

(1974); and *The Taxation of Industry: Fiscal Barriers to the Creation of Wealth* (1981). His several books on tax avoidance and evasion include *Tax Avoidance and Evasion: The Individual and Society* (1979).

For the IEA Dr Bracewell-Milnes has written 'The Economics of Tax Reduction', in *Taxation: A Radical Approach* (IEA Readings No.4, 1970); 'Market Control over Land-Use "Planning"', in *Government and the Land* (IEA Readings No.13, 1974); 'The Fisc and the Fugitive', in *The State of Taxation* (IEA Readings No.16, 1977); an Epilogue, 'Is Tax Avoidance/Evasion a Burden on Other Taxpayers?', in *Tax Avoision* (IEA Readings No.22, 1979); *Land and Heritage: The Public Interest in Personal Ownership* (Hobart Paper No.93, 1982); *The Wealth of Giving* (Research Monograph No.43, 1989); Introduction to *Which Road to Fiscal Neutrality?* (IEA Readings No.32, 1990); and 'Earmarking in Britain: Theory and Practice', in *The Case for Earmarked Taxes* (Research Monograph No.46, 1991).

John Chown was educated at Gordonstoun and Selwyn College, Cambridge (First Class Honours in Economics, Adam Smith Prize 1953, Wrenbury Scholarship 1954). He founded J.F. Chown and Company Limited in 1962. The company specialises in international tax, working out the strategic consequences of alternative business and financing strategies where the tax laws and practice of more than one country are involved. John Chown's special interest is the relationship between international tax, foreign currency fluctuations and international finance.

An active and extensive writer and lecturer on taxation and international finance, he was co-editor of the *Journal of Strategy in International Taxation* and was, for some years, the contributor to the *Financial Times* of a regular column, 'Taxation and the Investor'. His books include *Tax Efficient Foreign Exchange Management* (Woodhead-Faulkner, 1990). He is on the editorial committee of *Treasury Today*, published by the Institute of Chartered Accountants. For the IEA he wrote an Eaton Paper, *The Corporation Tax — a Closer Look* (1965), and, more recently, contributed a paper, 'European/British Company Taxation', to *The State of the Economy 1991* (IEA Readings No. 34, 1991).

A co-founder and Executive Committee member of the Institute for Fiscal Studies, John Chown is actively involved in tax policy issues in the UK, the EEC and elsewhere, and serves on the tax committee of the Institute of Directors, and on the London Committee of the International Fiscal Association.

Cedric Sandford is Professor Emeritus of Political Economy of the University of Bath and was formerly Director of the Bath University Centre for Fiscal Studies. He has published widely in professional journals and his recent books (written jointly) include *The Compliance Costs of Business Taxes in New Zealand* (1992), *Administrative and Compliance Costs of Taxation* (1989), *The Irish Wealth Tax* (1985), *Tax Policy-Making in the United Kingdom* (1983). He also wrote *Taxing Wealth in New Zealand* (1987). He has held visiting fellowships in the USA and Australia and has been a consultant to OECD, IMF, World Bank, United Nations, several overseas governments and the National Audit Office.

Professor Sandford is an IEA author of long standing, having written a Hobart Paper (No.32), *Taxing Inheritance and Capital Gains*, in 1965 (2nd Edn. 1967), and being joint author of a Research Monograph (No.34), *Grants or Loans?*, published in 1980.

Bruce Sutherland, CBE, FCA, is a chartered accountant who is well-known as a specialist in the theory and practice of the capital taxes. He was, for many years, Chairman of the Taxation Committees of the Institute of Directors and of the Association of British Chambers of Commerce and a member of that of the Confederation of British Industry. He is a long-standing member of the Addington Society.

Dr Ronald D. Utt is the Managing Director of Novecon Management Co. and a Principal of Novecon Ltd. (providing investment, trading, and consulting services for companies doing business in Eastern Europe).

Prior to joining Novecon, Dr Utt served as the Vice President and Chief Operating Officer of the National Chamber Foundation, the research and education affiliate of the US Chamber of Commerce. Under Dr Utt's direction the Foundation focussed its resources on studies covering tax reform for economic growth, social regulation, health care, privatisation and Central European economic reform.

Dr Utt also served as the co-director of the Bulgarian Economic Growth and Transition Project which took a team of 25 US businessmen and economic consultants to Bulgaria in 1990; it produced a 600-page blueprint for economic reform. Since then he has frequently consulted for Bulgaria's Ministry of Industry and Trade on industrial re-organisation and privatisation. He has also advised government officials in many other countries.

Prior to joining the National Chamber Foundation, Dr Utt was the John M. Olin Distinguished Fellow in Political Economy at the Heritage

Foundation, and before that, the Associate Director for Privatization at the US Office of Management and Budget during the Reagan administration. He also served as the US Chamber's Deputy Chief Economist and created and edited the *Journal of Economic Growth*.

Dr Utt received his PhD from Indiana University and his BS from Penn State University.